TOWARDS A NEW CONSCIOUSNESS

Towards a
New Consciousness

Dr. R. P. Kaushik

SENTIENT PUBLICATIONS

First Sentient Publications edition 2008
Copyright © 1973, 1978 by Dr. R. P. Kaushik

A paperback original

Cover design by Kim Johansen, Black Dog Design

Library of Congress Cataloging-in-Publication Data

Kaushik, R. P., 1926-1981
    Towards a new consciousness / R. P. Kaushik. – 1st Sentient Publications ed.
        p. cm.
    ISBN 978-1-59181-058-2
    1. Spiritual life. I. Title.

BL624.K37 2007
204'.4–dc22

                                            2007023765

Printed in the United States of America

10 9 8 7 6 5 4 3 2 1

SENTIENT PUBLICATIONS

A Limited Liability Company
1113 Spruce Street
Boulder, CO 80302
www.sentientpublications.com

In the early 1970s, several Western spiritual seekers in India encountered Dr. R.P. Kaushik (1926-1981), a physician living in an industrial town on the outskirts of New Delhi. Dr. Kaushik spoke of a transformation in consciousness, which he had undergone, and was exploring the nature and ramifications of his experience. To many Westerners, his open-ended inquiry resembled a Socratic dialogue, probing the nature of perception, thought and thinking, beliefs, and spiritual experience. From an Eastern perspective, his approach may have resembled that of Ramana Maharshi or J. Krishnamurti. And yet he did not refer to a personal teacher or to any other spiritual authority in his inquiry, and challenged all assumptions, including his own.

Although he was relatively unknown, Dr. Kaushik touched thousands of lives in both the West and the East, and appeared to have a deep and lasting influence on those who engaged with him, if even only for a single conversation. Dr. Kaushik's approach was a particularly freeing influence for those who were confused or disillusioned by the spiritual claims and goals being proposed by the various teachers or communities with which they had been involved. This influence came not only through the content and method of his dialogues, but also through a personal presence that bore witness to the depth of his understanding.

In the 1970s, cognitive scientists were just beginning to approach the study of mind and consciousness. Dr. Kaushik drew on this work, and his approach to self-inquiry also stands out as an early and original attempt to bring a scientific discipline to a first-person investigation into the nature of mental processes.

Up until his untimely death on July 15th, 1981, the Doctor (as he was affectionately known) traveled widely at the invitation of friends and students in Europe and America as well as his native India. In talks and conversations he shared his understanding tirelessly.

Dr. Kaushik wrote *Towards a New Consciousness* in India in 1973. Four subsequent books, which consisted of collective talks and conversations, were published by Journey Publications between 1976 and 1979 in America. When Journey reprinted this volume in 1979, Dr. Kaushik still felt that it represented "the essence of his discovery." As friends and former publishers of his books, we are pleased that Sentient has chosen to include *Towards a New Consciousness* in their series of spiritual classics, and that Dr. Kaushik's work can be introduced to new readers.

Because Dr. Kaushik expresses the essence of this understanding so eloquently in the preface to this volume, let us refer you directly to his own words.

Kent Babcock and Wendell Wallach
June 2007

Contents

Contents

Preface

This book is not the product of a well thought-out, logically coherent system or philosophy. It is the outcome of 'seeing' or perception from moment to moment. Therefore, it is not in the form of teaching or advice to the reader, because in that form it may mean very little—or it may mean something entirely different from what is intended. It is rather a thinking aloud which is audible only when the ear and the heart are open and the intellect is resting. Because of the nature of this writing, it may not be very acceptable from the literary point of view. There are repetitions which may appear superfluous, but this style is maintained for the sake of emphasis. The same words have been used to convey different meanings in different places. The chapters, which were written in a different chronological order from the one that appears in the book, have been arranged to produce a semblance of continuity. But the author conceived each chapter as an entity complete in itself.

To one reader this approach may appear very close to that of Shri J. Krishnamurti; to another it may appear to be a translation of the Yoga Sutras of Patanjali. But it is neither. When one sees or perceives, perception is integral or whole; it is neither this nor that. The Yoga Sutras have been given at the ends of the chapters when appropriate. They have been quoted not as authority in support of the author, but because when one sees, one sees a harmony behind even apparent contradictions. Perception is always new; it is always in the present. Tradition is old—but there would be no tradition if there were no truth entrapped in its core.

The human mind, in its search for psychological security, seizes upon this truth and organizes it. It is then rendered inert and fossilized. It is only the inexplicable power of perception which sets this truth free, and allows one to proceed further and avoid the pitfalls through which tradition has travelled.

While going through these pages, the reader is advised not to interpret or draw conclusions. To draw conclusions is the easiest thing to do. But if the reader understands, he will see what is behind these words. This understanding is not of the intellect; it comes only out of openness of the heart and complete attention.

For those who have no time to go through these pages patiently, the following synopsis can be given:

"See and listen but do not believe. Do not repeat what you do not understand. Be honest with yourself. With this honesty and simplicity in your heart, truth may knock at your door."

RPK
Delhi 1973

Meditation

To meditate is to find the meditator. Without discovering the meditator (the entity which wants to see God, truth or nirvana) meditation becomes an instrument of illusion: to find the meditator is to end it. The entity, the *I* which says I must find God or truth, will never find it. The intellect, being limited, cannot realize what is limitless or eternal. The highest realization the intellect can have is that it is limited and conditioned, and therefore incapable of seeing truth. The dawn of this understanding silences the intellect. The total silencing of the intellect is the ending of the meditator and also of meditation. The ending of meditation is the flowering of love.

If one is sensitive and serious, this flowering can be realized in this very instant. Otherwise one may have to go through various techniques and methods of meditation, and see their limitations. These methods and techniques are the products of the intellect and so perpetuate *I* and *me* in more subtle forms. Realization of the futility of any search for truth through these techniques is the beginning of wisdom.

An Approach to a New Consciousness

In order to look, find or discover something new, we have to give our complete attention to the object or question under observation. A mind full of disturbing thoughts, fears, anxieties and prejudices is incapable of looking at, and understanding, the meaning and significance of anything. Such a mind will only see what it wants to see and hear what it wants to hear. In short, such a mind is incapable of seeing anything objectively—whatever it sees is its own projection. Every human mind is heavily conditioned by its own past background and the history of the last million years. Therefore to 'see' or look, conditioning must come to an end.

In the search for a way to end conditioning, many systems of meditation have come into existence. Any system of meditation must answer the following two questions:

1. Is it possible for a human mind to go beyond its conditioning—that is, to be free of its hopes, fears, longings and prejudices?

2. In going beyond its own conditioning, is it possible for such a mind to remain free of any new conditioning?

The first question is answered affirmatively by many systems which aim at providing a new conditioning in place of the old. But most systems fail to answer the second question. This question is very important, and unless it is answered correctly, the human

1

problem cannot be adequately solved. Every conditioning, however satisfying, however new, will become old in the course of time and create the same problems for the mind. Life is ever changing and moving; its movement is forever creating new challenges. Unless a mind is totally free of all conditioning, it will be incapable of meeting these challenges and will inevitably come to conflict and sorrow. To satisfy these two criteria, any meditation must lead to a quality of mind which is not only free of prejudices, fears, and conflicts, but at the same time highly active, energetic and sensitive.

Most systems, by advocating certain techniques, beliefs and philosophy, aim at sublimating these urges and fears. But in the very pursuit of these techniques the mind loses its total energy and sensitivity.

Then how are we to come upon this quality of mind? Whenever we are interested in a new problem we can look at it seriously and earnestly. This very seriousness and earnestness creates an intensity, an energy which makes the mind quiet and purges it of its longings and urges. Perhaps the scientist, working in his laboratory, is in such a state of mind—in the technological field it may be easier to have this quality of perception and observation. But if we can look in the same earnest way at our own consciousness—our beliefs, ideas, fears and urges—the problem is solved.

In order to understand or find out if there is something called truth or God apart from the everyday mundane existence which is already known, such an energetic and quiet mind is the first prerequisite.

There are many ancient systems, and every other day we hear of a new brand of meditation which promises its followers a very quick, sure achievement of bliss and happiness. And each system claims to be exclusively authentic, stating that all the rest, if not spurious, are at least inadequate and unsuited to modern times.

Unfortunately, the world today is passing through an unprecedented moral and social crisis. Modern man, having rejected old values which are obviously obsolete, has been unable to find new moorings and is incapable of facing and meeting the exacting challenges of an ever-changing, complex modern life. Even with the highest technological advances, man is not able to cope with the increasing frustration created by the recent explosion of population. With growing material prosperity, discovery of newer and newer facts of life, and ever greater mastery over external nature, man is also piling up devastating means of self-destruction. There is an ever-increasing threat to his physical and psychological existence. This complexity has led to fragmentation of his personality and has resulted in the mounting incidence of neurosis, psychosis, suicide, crime and violence.

Under the ever-present threat of insecurity and frustration inherent in an outwardly rich and prosperous life, man today is in desperate need of a new faith, a new hope, and possibly a new way of life which can help him solve his problems of daily living and equip him to face the serious challenges of a complex modern life. Under such circumstances, he is eager to believe and follow any-one who promises him a quick and miraculous remedy. This is precisely the reason why any mind-manipulator with a hypnotic personality and a flair for salesmanship, aided by intensive prop-aganda and an army of publicity agents, is able to gather large crowds of followers. But after the initial enthusiasm common to any new venture, these followers are likely to become disil-lusioned. And then either they become totally cynical, or they again start building up hopes for the next messiah to come. Such a state of affairs only increases the confusion which already exists and offers no way out of the predicament.

There are many human beings today who are more interested in a new network of escapes than in solving the fundamental problems of life. Perhaps such people will always go on following one 'ism' or another, one leader or another, and must always belong to the latest group. But apart from these people, there is, though in a small minority at present, an ever-increasing number of serious-minded people who would like to investigate, seriously study, and experiment with whatever is presented to them. They will not accept anything *a priori*, as an article of belief or faith, without completely understanding its implications. Such readers are invited to share this investigation into the possibility of a new consciousness.

However, as things are now, it is only negatively that we can come upon the true meaning and significance of meditation, which is not a system or a method but a way of life—a way of looking and observing.

The Significance of Life

We are born, we grow and multiply, and then we decline and die. We attach so much importance to things and activities of life—we pursue them, possess them, and in this pursuit there is tremendous effort and struggle. But at the end we reach nowhere; death snatches everything away. Seeing this, we want to understand what all this is about. We want to understand the meaning and significance of life. We turn in various directions in our search, but what do we find?

Biology is the science of life, but it studies and describes only the outer, superficial activities of life. It describes the superficial differences between the living and the non-living, but all this does not tell us what life is, what its significance is. To proceed a little deeper we may develop the science of psychology, but psychology describes only the activities of mind, and that too does not take us very far. It does not tell us anything about the mainspring of mind. It tells us nothing about the origin and ending of thought. And so unsatisfied, we turn to parapsychology and explore the psychic field, or turn to mysticism to discover the solution to the riddle of life. In this endeavor we may find some satisfying answers, some ray of hope, some comfort or solace. But these answers are in conflict with reason and scientific thought, and so our mind remains divided. We cannot have an integrated outlook. What is the remedy? What are we to do? Is there any solution to this riddle, or are we doomed to a life of perpetual seeking and conflict?

In order to make our search or enquiry more meaningful, we

must first discover the true motive of our enquiry. What do we seek and why do we seek? We may have a natural intellectual curiosity, but that does not lead us very far. Intellectual curiosity is quite helpful in studying the various phenomena of life, but it can provide only intellectual answers to some of the profound problems of life—and such intellectual formulation does not solve anything fundamentally.

To find the meaning of life, we will have to turn to our own lives. What is the aim of any action or activity of our life? Is it not happiness or joy? In our innumerable activities of life, from morning till evening, from childhood to old age, are we not pursuing happiness? And in spite of this endless hectic activity, this strife and struggle, how many of us can say that we are truly happy? And why do we seek happiness? Do we seek something which we have or something which we do not have? We never seek that which we have, so when we seek happiness, does it not mean that we lack it? Some of us may have a sense of satisfaction in our lives—a certain sense of achievement or possession within the framework of an arbitrary goal. Normally, there is no permanent satisfaction. After a transient flash which we call satisfaction, boredom soon engulfs us, and we must pursue this satisfaction endlessly. This pursuit ultimately becomes a means of escape from boredom. If we do not want to continue this pursuit, we may cultivate a scale of observation which only looks downwards—we compare our lot with that of people who are less fortunate and privileged. But this satisfaction soon evaporates if we look upwards and compare ourselves with people who are more privileged. This contentment is no contentment at all, but only resistance and a sense of exclusion in our outlook. However, if instead of developing this mental resistance, we pursue pleasure and satisfaction endlessly in an uninhibited way, such a pursuit results in social problems as well as undermining our physical and mental health.

In the process of satisfying our organic needs, a certain amount of sensory pleasure is a natural and perhaps necessary accompaniment. It is not necessary to destroy these sensory pleasures—

methods such as those widely practised by the ascetics were nothing more than the cultivation of negative pleasure. At the physical level, sensory pleasure and pain may be performing a protective physiological function. But the separation of these sensory pleasures from the organic needs, and the exclusive pursuit of these pleasures, dulls the mind and destroys health. Whatever the extent of sensory pain may be, it is a problem with a comparatively easy solution: either it is cured, or if it is incurable, sooner or later death closes the chapter of misery. But when we derive psychological pleasure from these sensory pleasures, we build up an unending potential for psychological pain and sorrow at the same time—it appears to be unlimited in time and scope. Pleasure and pain appear to be diametrically opposed, but in fact they are very closely related. There is no absolute difference, only a relative one. On the physical plane, temperature and pressure applied to the skin are pleasurable at one point, but become painful above a certain degree. On the psychological level this difference is narrower, although ordinary human consciousness seldom perceives it. Psychological pleasure and pain are built upon their physical counterparts through the agency of thought. By dwelling on these pleasures for a length of time, desire is built up. The energy of desire is very destructive: first a desire clamors for its satisfaction, but the state of satisfaction is transient—and extremely so if the state of the mind is restless and agitated. There are occasions when this momentary satisfaction appears to be a very poor reward for its price of restlessness, anxiety and effort. We are inclined to feel the need to curb this desire, but in our struggle to curb or destroy it we make a tremendous effort and waste a lot of energy. If the mind is weak, we are likely to make resolves and pledges, only to break them eventually and face guilt feelings and conflict. If we are built of stronger fiber we may crush our desires by an effort of will, and thus dull our sensibilities and mutilate the personality. We may become so-called saints—with a placid, smiling countenance, yet with a restless burning inside. So desire is a double-edged sword— if we satisfy it, it leads to remorse and regret; if we suppress it, it leads to still greater turmoil and restlessness.

Desire has no end: it seeks more and more, almost always in a new setting. The repetitive satisfaction of desire in the same monotonous setting leads to boredom and frustration, so without a semblance of newness or creativity, the repetition of pleasure has sharply diminishing returns. And then the search for pleasure becomes the greatest sorrow of our lives. Seeing this conflict and dilemma, intellectuals like Bertrand Russell have advised means—based on intellectual considerations—to have trouble-free pleasure. His book "The Conquest of Happiness" is recommended for those who cannot take the trouble of going to the root of the problem, beyond intellectual solutions. For serious and earnest people who would like to solve the problem fundamentally, his solutions are too facile and full of contradictions to be of much real value.

In the physical world, pleasure and pain are to a great extent concrete and tangible, whereas in the psychological world they are based completely upon notion or thought. Thought is flexible and capable of moving rapidly in opposite directions. It may not always correspond to objective reality. Indeed it can divorce itself from reality and become completely hypothetical and imaginary. Such thought can be a source of great torture and conflict and may result in endless misery. Therefore thought as pleasure must be understood and dissolved before it can function rationally and sanely on the physical level in our lives.

Apart from the pain which we build up through our thought process, and for which we are directly responsible, there is another kind of sorrow which we have to face while living in this unkind, brutal and competitive world. We may have talent and capacities, but they are often neither recognized nor encouraged unless we have influential backing. Neither talent nor proficiency, but recommendation, becomes the highest qualification. This leads to great heartache and frustration. The cunning and the dishonest apparently succeed and flourish, while the good and the noble fail and suffer. So there is the sorrow of not succeeding. And yet, even if some of us are lucky enough to succeed economically, we still feel lonely in this selfish world, because more often than not we are exploited in the name of friendship and love. So there is the sorrow of not being loved, or of losing loved ones through death or desertion. Bereft of any genuine love and friendship, there is a great gap, a great vacuum or void in our lives, and this brings us terrible fear or boredom. We are always escaping from it in different directions, through the various avenues of amusements, drugs or sex. This escape may take the form of a pursuit of images and ideals, such as the worship of name, fame and prestige, or ideals of social and humanitarian activity. On the highest scale of values, escape may take the form of living and dying for a cause, living as an instrument of God's will, or living a life of meditation in search of the truth and glory that is God. And finally if we do succeed in pursuing any one of these highest escapes exclusively and continuously, the mind may become concentrated in one direction and yet remain dull and insensitive in other areas. And sorrow pursues us in the form of this dullness—we lose the chance to understand the significance of life.

We know nothing about the total energy of life; we know only the fragmentary energy of desire which moves us in everyday life. When desire is satisfied, there is a momentary flash of happiness or pleasure, followed by a relatively long period of boredom or depression. Every stimulation is followed by depression, and rapidly repeated stimulation will eventually lead to exhaustion and decay.

The more pleasure is pursued, the more the underlying boredom is intensified. So a life given to an endless search for pleasure becomes very superficial and colorless. Boredom is perhaps the essential feature of our ordinary, everyday life—there seems to be no escape from it. Any search for a remedy for boredom only invites and intensifies sorrow. Are we to accept sorrow and compromise with it? Or are we to extol sorrow, sing its praises by raising it to the poetic level? Or are we to worship sorrow as a great blessing, as some religious orders have done in the past? No doubt sorrow has always acted as a catalyst in urging men to newer heights. Much poetry and other fine arts have sprung from sorrow. Pleasure and satisfaction lull us to complacency and sleep. It is the great challenge of sorrow which endows us with an awareness which alone can help us to advance to new dimensions. It is therefore necessary to understand the energy of sorrow. In the past, men have devised innumerable escapes from sorrow, but never completely understood it, and therefore they could not transform it.

In order to understand the significance and meaning of life, two things are absolutely essential. First, we must say goodbye to all those philosophies which insist on narrowing the field of sense perception, and indirectly preach the dulling of senses. To discover something new and vast, we need a heightened sensitivity and sense perception. The senses should be trained to operate fully and completely, without any inhibitions and yet without indulgence. Second, we must reject all methods of escape from sorrow, pay full attention to sorrow and see if it can be transformed.

We have seen that the search for happiness only brings sorrow. Does this mean that there is no real happiness in life? If we reflect on our lives, we see that there are some rare moments in which quite unexpectedly there is a great sense of vastness, beauty and delight, apparently without any cause—not the result of any achievement, possession, or satisfaction of our desires. This sense of delight may come to us while looking at a beautiful face, a sunset with a beautiful play of colors on the clouds in the sky, or a starry night with the full moon casting her glory on the earth. It may come to us while we are standing in the doorway of a carriage of a fast moving train, when the fields and trees are running quickly past our eyes and our whole life appears so trivial and transient. It may happen when a gentle breeze blows, touches gently on our face, and the leaves and flowers dance merrily with the rhythm of the breeze. Or delight may come to us while hearing a temple or a church bell, or while standing in front of an idol or statue. It was while looking at a temple idol that the proud and arrogant Pundit Nimai was suddenly transformed into the humble and devoted

Chaitanya Maha Prabhu. This could happen in different ways, and yet the same environment and same situation will not always bring about the same experience. This joy cannot be repeated. It is not the culmination of any particular desire or search. A moment before we do not know what is coming. Face to face with a totally new and unexpected situation, the mind becomes completely still and silent. The next moment there is a flash, an explosion; our ego is burst asunder and there it is—this creative joy.

Creative joy is a spontaneous happening. It must happen to us, it must come to us; we cannot pursue it. It comes to us in those unexpected moments when the mind is still, calm and free from all expectations. A life of joy can be a life of spontaneity, but a life of strife, struggle, and pursuit is a life of sorrow. Pleasure can be pursued, and the endless pursuit of pleasure brings boredom, exhaustion, decay and sorrow. But joy cannot be pursued and cultivated—it is a spontaneous happening. Every pleasure is built up around the central core of an experience of joy, through thought and memory, and so pleasure cannot be destroyed without destroying that core of joy. Many ascetics have tried to destroy or curb pleasure, but have only succeeded in building up a negative pleasure of ego, and a dryness of heart. By asceticism we may destroy positive pleasure, but at the same time we destroy the possibility of joy ever coming into our lives. True understanding of the nature and limitations of pleasure must bring our search for pleasure to an end, leaving our mind in a state of silence. It is in this state of being that joy blossoms. It is joy alone which can transform our minds. Joy is the Divine Grace, if we choose to use that term, which does not necessarily come to righteous and moral people, but may even touch the lives of low or so-called immoral people. Joy shines in its full glory in the lives of simple and humble people. There are no preconditions for its visit, but there is one condition for its blossoming. That condition is true humility. The arrogance of righteous or austere moral living, of book learning or knowledge of scriptures, is the greatest hurdle.

When we face sorrow, understand it and transform it, we may

understand what love is. The flowering of love is the ending of sorrow, the ending of the search for the significance and meaning of life. Awareness of sorrow is the beginning of the question, and the beginning of love is the ending of all questions. A mind in a state of love asks no questions. Understanding sorrow is meditation, and the blossoming of love is the ending of meditation.

Freedom

Freedom has been variously interpreted and understood by different people at different times. There was a time, at least in the East, when freedom implied going beyond the cycle of birth and death. As it was then presumed, all the miseries and sorrow of human life originated with the birth of man. But if we go deeply into this question and its implications, we must conclude that much of this sorrow is the result of imagination and thought. At the time of birth, we do not suffer from serious pain, nor is nine months of life in the womb of the mother a nightmarish experience for the fetus—though it may be so in the adult imagination. In the same way, our fear of death is the result of thought or imagination: when death comes, the dying person seldom consciously experiences serious suffering. If a man could live in peace and harmony all his life, without conflict and sorrow, he would not mind being born again and again. Rebirth might be a matter of eternal joy for such a person—death would lose its horror for him and sorrow would be a word foreign to his consciousness.

But such an approach to the enormous problems of life—pursuing a *nirvana* or *moksha* beyond the cycle of life and death—means at least a partial escape or withdrawal into a state which is beyond the pale of everyday existence. For some religious sects, a renunciation of worldly life, which was a natural corollary of this way of thinking, became the *sine qua non* of moksha or salvation. In following this course, some individuals may have found a solution to their individual problems, but for the large mass of humanity,

13

this has been impossible. This approach could not meet the challenges of day-to-day life in its totality. The total human problem—as opposed to the individual problem—has remained unsolved.

What then is freedom? Freedom has always been linked with necessity. One would like to give expression to one's urges, desires and ideas, but one may come into conflict with one's social environment. However, if a man conforms to the social code, he may come into conflict with himself. No social code is sacrosanct; it is liable to change in response to challenges from individuals or groups of individuals. An individual will have to discover how far in his non-conformity he can go without inviting reactions from others in a social organization, and even if such non-conformity is really necessary for him to live in freedom. The common revolt of the individual against social tyranny and oppression is a reaction, and it does not bring about freedom—because reaction only invites further reaction, and thus an endless chain of reactions is set in motion. In the psychological and social sphere, reaction is closely linked with its opposite. Violence has often been met with violence in history and it has not ended violence. Even non-violence has not eliminated violence. Thousands of wars have been fought to end and abolish war, but war has not been abolished. Pacifism has been preached as a remedy, but it cannot be of much avail unless man eradicates greed, violence and competition from his inner nature. The seeds of war and social conflict are sown in the individual human psyche. Unless human nature is radically transformed, the preaching and practising of outer remedies and systems will not bring an end to conflict.

So we must understand, not as a creed or a dogma but actually—through our own observation and understanding, which we may call meditation—that reaction, far from being freedom, is a very superficial response of a superficial mind.

Conflict begins in the individual human psyche, and as long as that inner conflict is not eliminated, no society built by individuals in conflict will ever be free of conflict and chaos. An individual, after all, is not isolated from the mass of total human consciousness, and in bringing about a change in himself he influences the entire human psyche. Therefore, freedom implies not only an outer environment which is conducive to change, but also an inner state free from fear, anxiety and sorrow.

This state free from inner conflict cannot be brought about by affluence and material progress—rather these conditions have aggravated the inner conflict. Man must turn inwards to find the seeds of conflict within his own psyche, and see the different fragments. In this observation, which is meditation, perhaps he may bring about the integration of his personality. In the process he may break through the shackles of the environment to find his freedom immediately, in the present, not in some distant future or after his death. Freedom after death is a concept which has very little meaning or significance.

Freedom does not lie simply in being free to do what we like. We may do whatever we like in a chain of reactions, with a restless, agitated mind, and yet this implies the negation of freedom. If we trace our actions back to their very source, we can easily find out how the subconscious, by providing hidden urges and motivations and by molding our habits, denies us the spontaneous action which springs from freedom and leads again towards freedom. Freedom, therefore, is not from something external. It is a state of being—free from past conditioning and subconscious motivations and urges. Such a state can proceed only from a silent meditative mind, a mind which is full of energy, love and compassion.

Unitive action cannot come merely from intellect or reasoning, or any urge or emotion, or even intuition—which after all may be self-oriented. This action proceeds from the highest intelligence and integration, which is the bedrock of a silent meditative mind.

Such a mind is non-conforming because it is its own authority, not dependent on outside sources, either persons or books, for guidance—not depending even on its own past experience, except perhaps negatively inasmuch as it does not repeat a past mistake. It does not act according to a pattern, an idea, system or philosophy. Such a mind observes and understands. Out of that observation and understanding, action takes place which does not breed conflict and sorrow, for it is born out of insight and intelligence.

> *"Ritambhara tatra prajna."*
> —Patanjali; Yoga Sutras I:48

> *"In that state intelligence is free of uncertainty and doubt."*

Spontaneity

From the ancient Chinese sage Lao-Tzu to the most modern thinker, many have talked of spontaneity. There is no doubt that there cannot be any freedom without spontaneity. But the word spontaneity is not spontaneity. Without understanding the whole implication of the word, superficial or mechanical responses may be confused with spontaneity.

It is obvious that an action which proceeds from thought is not spontaneous. Even when the intellect is silent, is an action, springing from emotion, inclination or habit, spontaneous? Can an action proceeding from animal instincts and urges be spontaneous? Can that which is spontaneous for a dog also be spontaneous for a man? Barking at other dogs and chasing them away may be very normal for a dog—but if a man starts doing the same to other human beings can it be termed normal or spontaneous?

Man has inherited many blind urges and instincts from his animal ancestors during the course of evolution. Is blind imitation of the animal kingdom possible for man? Can he act instinctively without conflict? Whenever man acts like an animal, can he really act without rationalization, justification or condemnation? Does he not always use the intellect even when he behaves or tries to behave like an animal? To come to spontaneity, man must not only go beyond conscious thought but at the same time beyond the thought buried in the subconscious as memory and blind urges.

Any forcible excision of thought—by effort of will, concentration, or any other method of exclusion—will not bring man to a state of spontaneity, but only to a state of reduced sensitivity or resistance. Continued practice of a method or system which suppresses certain parts of the mind may bring about a state of great energy by eliminating conscious conflict. Perhaps certain normally difficult activities may become automatic or mechanical. But such an automatic or mechanical action cannot be truly spontaneous; automation is not spontaneity. Therefore to discover spontaneity it is necessary for conscious and unconscious thought to come to an end out of observation and understanding, and not as a result of outer discipline. Only through the ending of thought can one come face to face with spontaneity.

Spontaneity springs from a silent meditative mind. Spontaneity is creative. The intellect must stop its own creation and projection if creative spontaneity is to operate. This also means that spontaneity cannot be pursued, since the pursuit of spontaneity is an intellectual process. Artists and poets have glimpses of this creative state, but in the effort to recapture this state they lose it. It is easy for spontaneity to come to human beings, but it is difficult to stay in this state. It requires tremendous discipline, and part of that discipline is not to pursue the creative state.

The sensitive mind of a poet or artist is a mirror in which this creative energy may be reflected. A poet or artist is not necessarily one who writes or paints, but simply one who is sensitive. To stay in this state of spontaneity, the mind must be simple and sensitive. This sensitivity is destroyed by drugs. Those drugs may be soft or hard, or they may be the powerful drugs of pride, ambition or greed. A proud, ambitious or greedy mind is violent and distorted; such a mind cannot be still and quiet. Without silence spontaneity cannot manifest.

In the ordinary human mind there is conflict between thought and action. Some have tried to eliminate this conflict by inhibiting or suppressing thought by one method or another. Under such circumstances, there is a free play of unregenerate nature without hindrance. The conflict disappears but imbalance remains. But when the intellect becomes silent as a result of great

watchfulness and understanding, the mind undergoes a transformation. Basic human nature changes. This transformation is
deep and penetrating; it proceeds from above downwards or
from within outwards. First the intellectual conditioning goes and
the intellect is illumined. It is no longer a restless, confused, self-
centered instrument employed for rationalizing and justifying
instinctive behavior. It becomes a clear, unconfused agent, thinking sanely and logically in the higher light of all-integrating intelligence. When the energy of transformation touches the obscure
animal urges, they are transformed, and a new human being is
born. Many people have come upon spontaneity in some rare
moments, but very few indeed live in it. To live in it is to know its
great power and beauty. All other powers are based on friction
and conflict and are therefore ugly. This is a supreme power
which is beauty at the same time. To discover and live a life of
spontaneity, one must turn one's back on all the wealth and riches
that hand or intellect can create—worldly riches or inward riches
of intellectual knowledge or psychic powers. Then being completely empty and full of humility, one is in a state in which spontaneity can come and begin a true creation—a creation which is
not touched by time, and so is free of decay and death.

To be in a state of spontaneity, one has to learn the supreme
art of self-surrender and live from moment to moment. One has
to learn to give up intellectual effort and cultivation of will, to be
just a watcher and a witness. In such a state all our burdens and
cares are taken up by the Supreme Energy and miracles happen
in our lives uninvited. One may call this supreme creative state by
any name, whether God, Beauty or Truth, but there is really no
energy greater than true spontaneity.

The ending of all search is the beginning of spontaneity. In a
state of spontaneity, one may do what one likes and there will be
no conflict, no error. Spontaneity is love. When there is love in
one's heart one can do no wrong. To discover spontaneity is to go
beyond social or conventional morality. To be spontaneous is to be
virtuous. A virtue which blossoms without any code or cause is the
only virtue.

Drug & Sex Experiences

Throughout the ages, drugs and sex have been used extensively to expand human consciousness to experience reality or truth. In the case of drugs, the stimulation experienced is a spurious one, because it is the result of a release phenomenon dependent upon the depression of the higher cerebral centers. In the same way, methods of concentration and so-called meditation are also dependent upon the depression and partial inhibition of the cerebral cortex and a selective release of the sub-cortical centers of the brain. The same psychic opening obtained through the rigorous and prolonged disciplines of the different yogic cults can be achieved in a much shorter time with the aid of drugs, given a competent guide and a serious aspirant. However the possible injurious side-effects of drugs may outweigh their advantages.

The proponents of modern systems of meditation condemn drugs vociferously. But there is evidence that alcohol, cannabis and charas were extensively used in the sadhana of one sect of tantrics in medieval times in India. And the highest ancient authority on yoga, Patanjali, was very candid and forthright in his treatise on yoga:

> "*Janmausadhi mantra tapah samadhija siddhaya.*"
>
> —Patanjali; IV:1
>
> "*Attainment of powers can come through birth, through drugs, or through mantra, discipline and self-absorption (samadhi).*"

In modern literature, Aldous Huxley has dealt with the theme of drugs and sex with the almost uncanny insight of a yogi or mystic. He has elaborated this theme at great length in his novel "Island" and to a lesser degree in "Doors of Perception" and "Brave New World". Many of his other novels touch upon these mystic themes. In modern Indian literature, these topics have been dealt with in a masterly manner by the noted tantric scholar Kaviraj Gopi Nath.*

In many of the old systems of yogic culture and mysticism, both Eastern and Western, great emphasis was also placed on controlling the sexual energy in order to attain psychic powers. This emphasis must have arisen because out of all the temptations to which the human mind is susceptible, sexual temptation is perhaps the most irresistible and formidable, due to its special status as a means of total self-abandon and self-absorption. Another aspect of the sexual instinct is that it is charged with procreative energy, and as such it was assumed that indulgence in sex is not only a sin but a great waste or drain of energy. The sexual act, if freed of conflict, is no more a waste of energy than any other physiological act; rather it is the conflict and guilt feeling built up around it which leads to a tremendous waste of energy.

The condemnation of sex was common not only to the medieval ascetics; even in modern times the great thinker and yogi Shri Aurobindo could not escape this way of thinking. He condemned sexual experience to the extent that he made no distinction between the sexual act with one's own wife and with a woman other than one's wife. He strictly enjoined all his sadhakas to eschew sexual experience, although he speaks of a state of self-realization in which the sexual act may not have any adverse effect. But it is not easily understandable how a sadhaka who has become so conditioned with sexual inhibitions will one day, after self-realization, suddenly find himself enjoying a sexual act without conflict.

*Bhartiya Sanskriti aur Sadhana.

Aware of all these implications, the Vam Marg tantrics used sexual symbology and the actual sexual act to go beyond these inhibitory influences so that their sadhana could be freed from many inner conflicts right from the beginning. Perhaps this tantric sadhana resulted in less conflict, self-torture and suppression, as it always took into consideration the conscious and subconscious urges of the aspirant, and the path or discipline was prescribed accordingly. The need for freedom was realized to be at the outset, and not at the end of the sadhana.

At present many young people in the West are trying to experiment with drugs and sex without controlled and perfected guidance. Perhaps these people are working under a handicap when compared with the tantrics, who had a well-developed technique and a complete philosophy. For most of these young people the risk of such experiments going astray and the chances of a consequent psychic trauma are great. In spite of these handicaps, many of these people have been able to go beyond drugs towards a true spiritual journey.

Now what is the value of these experiences, or for that matter of any experience? Drugs like mescaline, LSD or hashish, by inhibiting certain higher centers of the brain and stimulating certain centers in the midbrain, may reveal the unconscious to the subject, or present before him a new set of values in place of the old one. But how is one to adopt these new values in a normal sober condition of mind, and not only under the continuous influence of the drug? If one could, after discovering these alternate values through insight into one's unconscious, adopt them and make them part of one's life without the need for further drugging, perhaps a great achievement could take place. But the greater and greater dependence on drugs—both for further experience and also in order to stabilize experience—leads to drug addiction rather than to spiritual awakening and insight. Reality, truth or bliss based or dependent on drugs is a chemical illusion, quite different from the release and freedom which come spontaneously out of attentive observation and awareness of life, inner as well as outer.

Similarly, a total sexual outlet may under certain circumstances reveal to the human mind an egoless state of spontaneous creativity or bliss—but the danger is that the mind may identify this state exclusively with the sexual experience. This creative or blissful state may come about through sex, but every sexual experience will not bring it about. The chances are that if we seek this state through these experiences, all that we will experience will be nothing more than sensation or repetitive stimulation—which will ultimately degenerate into sensual pursuit rather than the experience of creative release. If we learn the devastating mischief of ego and ego-building activities from such an experience, and at the same time also learn that freedom and creativity come out of the dissolution of the ego—not necessarily through sex—then we have laid the right basis for understanding the self and its destructive activities, and at the same time for transcending it.

The value of an experience lies not in what it gives us but in the opportunity it offers us to understand the limitation of an experience, and thus do away with the need for seeking further experience. Every person, from the most foolish to the most learned, from the most worldly to the most spiritual, talks of his experience. Everyone builds authority on experience—and it is this authority of experience which blocks listening and observation. The organization of experience leads to the fossilization and mechanization of mind, and destroys all possibility of creative reality reflecting through such a mind. Then what is one to do?

The highest truth, after all, is negative in character, and it is not possible to realize it through an experience but only by transcending experience and going to a state of non-experience. Unless experiences are critically evaluated, the danger inherent in all sadhanas and disciplines is that instead of experiencing truth and reality, one may lapse into a mechanical state of sensation-mongering.

Even in evaluating the highest tantric philosophy, it must be realized that a system or theory is based on certain facts at a given moment, and cannot reflect the entire truth, which is the whole of life. Pursuit of these systems may bring about great results and much satisfaction and profit; however, the real question is whether it is possible to realize truth by following any system, however elaborate. Truth is not only transcendental but also immanent; it is not static or fixed but viable, ever moving, immeasurable. Could that supreme, boundless energy be within the scope of any system, however profound and appealing? Could it be possible to understand life through any formula or method, except through extreme watchfulness, alertness and awareness from moment to moment as life proceeds and unfolds itself?

Life and a formula are irreconcilable. This is precisely why previous systems, methods of meditation, and spiritual disciplines failed lamentably to solve the ever-evolving problems of life, or to bring about a transformation in the human mind. Transformation only takes place when the mind can go beyond all systems and philosophies, live with the truth of life as it unfolds itself from moment to moment, and communicate directly with that truth.

Here a word of warning is necessary. The highest truth may be best described by *"neti, neti"* (not this, not this), the formula of ancient Hindu wisdom—but it must be borne in mind that human life is not negative in character. It is situated on the borderline of negative and positive, the meeting point of the material and the spiritual. Man walks with his feet firmly planted on the ground and with his head held in the sky.

Moreover, as one goes deeply into meditation, one sees that at various levels there is a movement from negative to positive and vice versa. Truth is dynamic and is always moving from negative to positive—in an endless, unfettered movement. At the level of the human consciousness, the human mind divides positive from negative, pleasure from pain, and joy from sorrow. It is this division, this fragmentation, which is the cause of sorrow—not karma or the cycle of birth and death. The separation of life from death is the cause of suffering, rather than the fact of life or death itself. It is this unity, this integration which is the final aim of true meditation, not the achievement of some hypothetical state of negative or positive truth. Systems and their pursuit may lead to a conclusion, a goal, a summit of the highest nirvana or *maha shunya*. By ardent practice one may remain fixed in one such region, but such a practice is the negation of truth, the fossilization of the human mind at its highest point. Truth is moving, dynamic and living, and only a mind which is living and active can keep up with the movement of truth. Perfection is not an image or an idea, but the capacity to move endlessly with every current, both positive and negative, of truth. This is the eternal dance of Natraj Shiva (the negative) with Mahamaya (the positive). It is most perfectly symbolized by the ancient Indian seers in the Shiva lingam. It may also be visualized as a pyramid or a triangle with its apex pointing upwards. The two sides meeting at the apex symbolize the unity of negative and positive, which at the base are so widely separated. As one goes higher and higher, the two opposites meet and create a harmony. In tantric symbology, this is beautifully represented by Tripur Sundari seated in the lap of Param Shiva; or by the highest manifestation of Lord Shiva as Ardhanarishwara, who is half male and half female.

To visualize this level or perceive it intuitively is one thing, but to experience it and actually live at that level is another. The highest aim of true meditation is to discover this dimension and live in it.

Experience and
Non-Experience

Life is an unbroken series of experiences; to live is to experience. There is no moment of life which is not an experience—there are more experiences in life than the mind is capable of coping with. Yet the mind is forever running in search of more experiences, deeper experiences, and so-called spiritual experiences. Is this a search for new experiences, or is it a search for more satisfying experiences? Is there a new experience at all? Can a conditioned mind experience anything new?

Throughout our lives, we are confronted with innumerable situations and events. Do we experience them or do we simply react to them? Can a mind in a state of reaction experience anything except perhaps its own reaction? Perhaps it does not even experience its own reaction fully. The moment such a reaction is sharp and disturbing, the mind avoids it or tries to run away from it through various cleverly cultivated means of escape. The mind is in a constant state of escaping instead of experiencing. Unfortunately in most cases it is not even aware of its escaping, and so this endless escaping continues. This escaping we call life. This escaping we call experience.

To experience anything completely, the mind must be totally calm and empty. When the mind is completely purged of its memories and longings, real experience can take place. In such a state, the experiencer is completely absorbed in the experienced—the subject and the object are one. When the experiencer does not have a separate existence, is there a memory, recognition or identification? Is one experience different from another? Is there a division between high and low, spiritual and profane? Is not every experience the same? When an absorbing experience is over, one becomes aware of a revitalizing freshness in the mind and body. Interpretation begins, and the experiencer emerges and strengthens itself. This interpretation is in terms of past conditioning and past experiences. The new is absorbed by the old and the new experience is dead.

So in any experience there are three stages: the first stage is complete absence of the experiencer. There is no trace of memory in this state and so in a way it is a state of non-experience; it is a negative state. The second stage is the state of after-effect in which there is an awareness of freshness and bliss. This is the positive state of experience. The third stage is the state of recognition and interpretation. This is the most destructive stage; the new is falsified and destroyed. In every experience there is a central core of truth around which a thick fabric of false is woven. In a conditioned mind the first two stages are momentary or completely absent—only the third is present. There is hardly any experience, only a repetition of sensation or a projection of memory. Therefore such a mind goes through life, through innumerable experiences, blindfolded and experiencing nothing. It is a dead mind, mechanically repeating itself like a tape recorder. Such a mind feels bored to death, and out of this horrible boredom, it seeks new experiences. This kind of seeking becomes another escape from life, and therefore denies one the possibility of having any true experience. Experience cannot be sought; it happens. What can be sought is not experience but sensation. Sensation pursued and repeated leads to dissipation and boredom.

Bored and dissatisfied with sensory pleasures, the mind seeks abiding pleasures, it seeks spiritual experiences. It divides experiences into worldly and spiritual, and then the search for spiritual experiences becomes a new form of greed and self-satisfaction. The human mind is capable of inventing great myths, and a mind bent upon seeking spiritual experiences creates them. A greedy mind is a petty mind. It worships its own creations—its own projections—as reality. Such a mind is caught in an endless illusion.

In the purely physical or technological field a certain amount of accumulation is necessary, but even in technological learning humility is essential if one wishes to be human and not mechanical. If status is not built upon the accumulation of technological experience, then this accumulation does not create a problem. But in the psychological field, the very accumulation of experience is the strengthening of the experiencer, the building of ego. The ego is very destructive, for it denies the possibility of true experiencing. So mechanical or physical memory can operate, but psychological interpretation of the pleasant and unpleasant must end for true experience to take place. When interpretation as pleasant and unpleasant ends, the mind is clean and innocent. When seeking ends, the mind is simple and free of greed. Such a mind is ready for benediction: truth comes to such a mind uninvited.

When the mind is free of memories and seeking, it is in an extremely heightened state of sensitivity: it is still and calm. Innumerable experiences pass through such a mind leaving no trace, no scar of memory. Such a mind is holy and unfragmented. When the experiencer and the experienced are one, there is no memory; memory is the remnant of an incomplete experience. The maturing height of an experience is non-experience. Non-experience is total freedom.

Experience is not pleasure; the search for pleasure through an experience is the denial of that experience. Experience is not satisfaction; a satisfying experience is an unabsorbed sensation. Stimulation brought about by an emotion, thought or drug, is a reaction, not an experience, and reaction does not bring freedom. The value of an experience lies in opening up the possibility of learning and self-knowledge. To see experience as non-experience is the height of understanding.

Faith

Faith implies belief in an object or phenomenon without proof. A person who so believes must have a very simple mind, a childlike innocence. Only in such innocence can faith really flourish and attain its full bloom. And faith can certainly perform miracles, because thought surcharged with emotion and simplicity has great power.

Faith has solved many problems of the human mind in the past. The avatars and gurus of old preached the way of faith, and most people accepted their teachings. But during the last two centuries there has been great progress in science and rational thought. The human mind has expanded its frontiers to domains hitherto unknown. These scientific and technological advances have influenced human life in all areas, and particularly in the religious sphere. Faith which insists on acceptance without proof cannot answer many of the questions posed by the rational way of life, and thus there has been a virtual collapse of all the values which were based on faith. The human mind has been unable to formulate any new values which can harmonize reason with faith. Like a boat without a rudder in uncharted waters, the human mind is facing the greatest crisis of our times—a crisis of con-sciousness.

In recent times, some self-styled avatars and gurus have pro-claimed new faiths, and it appears that the number of their fol-lowers is increasing at a rapid rate. The frustrated human mind is ready to clutch at any straw, and thanks to the magic of the mass

media, of publicity and propaganda, there appears to be a re-
surgence of religious feeling. But unless the tempo is kept up by
ceaseless propaganda and brainwashing, this enthusiasm is not
likely to endure. Sooner or later, the gnawing whisperings of
reason and doubt will erode these newly-founded sects and
philosophies.

To meet these challenges, some sects have tried to explain
metaphysics by scientific theories, but these theories are no more
than pseudo-science. Total reality or absolute truth will forever
remain beyond the pale of intellect and hence beyond science and
logic—for the simple reason that a fragment, however bright and
large, cannot encompass the whole.

What is the remedy then?

Obviously the remedy lies not in some new formula or philosophy, but in an earnest exercise of reason to discover the ultimate
limit of reason. It is only when the mind has exercised itself fully,
and exhausted all the light that reason is capable of providing,
that it can come to rest in silence. It is only in this silence that
reality is likely to be reflected. Having come face to face with this
reality, truth, beauty, God or whatever else one might like to call it,
man can discover the mainspring of a new faith—a new way of
religious life, free from sectarian bigotry, which will unite human
beings in a common bond of love and understanding. Such a
faith—based not on hearsay or second-hand experience but on
direct perception, which transcends but does not contradict
human reason—can be the foundation of the future religious life
of humanity.

In other words, instead of faith based on simple and unqual-
ified acceptance, this new faith must be based on incessant questioning, which implies a tremendous capacity for doubt. Previously, faith came out of an intuitive awareness; now it must be
built upon deep insight and thorough understanding. It will
begin with self-awareness and self-knowledge, and find its climax
in complete and perfect action and total freedom. Such an integral faith, which no amount of reasoning can destroy, must be the

faith of the present age and beyond. The discovery of such a faith is the aim of true meditation.

We are left with two possibilities. One is to have the highest concept, which is God, and realize that concept by faith, simplicity and a continuous, ardent approximation or identification. The results can be marvelous and gratifying, but one is only realizing the truth of one's own concept or conceptual truth. The other possibility is the way of incessant enquiry, of rejection of all that is known. Thereby we may come upon a silence in which absolute truth may manifest itself. As has been mentioned earlier, the direct and shortest route, if a route it may be called, is through direct perception, questioning and rejection. However, such an approach to reality demands rejection of all words and symbols. Moreover, it requires a great intensity, sensitivity, and insatiable discontent, along with a tremendous spirit of revolt. If we do not have or want to have all these qualities, the only alternative possible is to create the highest concept of God as love and beauty, and aspire to it through single-minded devotion. If we have accumulated outward wealth in the form of money, prestige and social position, or inward wealth in the form of belief in books, mantras and images, and we are not prepared to turn our back on these accumulations, we will then have only this method as a resort. It is just possible that as in the course of time we perceive the power of faith and the true imperishable riches faith can bring, that the hold of material and psychological wealth on our mind may decrease and we may be able to aspire to the highest concept. And perhaps if we are really fortunate we may come out of all this, and go beyond this highest concept into total freedom.

The Highest Concept

Devotees often ask this question: "I have faith in God but it is weak—it is not a steady flame. I have been sitting in contemplation; I have been repeating a mantra, but my mind wanders. What is the way to have single-minded devotion?" The first thing to understand is that real interest creates concentration. If we are intensely interested in a thing, the mind never wanders. If we have real faith, real love for our conceptual image, the mind will never wander. The trouble with most people is that in their conscious mind they have faith in God, but in their unconscious mind they have innumerable conflicting attachments. If devotion is to flourish, devotees must clear their unconscious minds of these conflicting attachments. In this way they will understand their unconscious minds and harmonize them with their conscious minds, and progress rapidly in the realization of their highest concept.

As far as possible, a specific time should be set aside for *sadhana*. A separate small room or corner of a room, free of noise and disturbance, is desirable. A cool and refreshing bath may be an aid in relaxing the mind and body, though it is not essential. Then sit in any convenient posture, with the spine and head erect, and begin by taking deep rhythmic breaths and concentrate the mind on them. These deep breaths will give extra oxygen to the brain and ward off fatigue and laziness, and at the same time help to relax the mind. While taking deep breaths watch the mind, and you will find that as long as breathing is deep and regular, the mind does not wander.

Now proceed to the second step. Stop concentrating on the breath and let the unconscious mind assume charge of this deep, regular breathing. If one has been repeating a mantra and wishes to continue with it, it should not be repeated mechanically and hurriedly. Instead, mentally pronounce the mantra, but with a sonorous musical rhythm. This musical rhythm is important, because feeling is naturally and easily associated with music. Try not only to listen to this musical note but also to feel its vibrations with the entire body, mind and being. If you have gone this far correctly, you will find that the mind does not wander. The mind becomes one with these waves of music.

One can go on indefinitely in this state, but let us not pursue it beyond the mind's saturation point—perhaps more than fifteen minutes in the beginning. Now there is no wandering of mind, there is peace and harmony. At this point the conscious and unconscious minds have given up their life-long conflict and are at peace with each other. Our highest concept, our deity, is the highest point of the unconscious mind, which we may call the superconscious. Now we are in communion with that power. Let us not be afraid of it. Let us not look upon it with awe and fear. It is part of our being, part of our mind, and we must have a relationship of harmony and oneness with this power. Fear of God is a very destructive concept. God is love, and fear is the isolation, the separateness from that power.

Having come to this state of harmony and peace, wait patiently in an attitude of expectancy for this power to communicate. This communication may come in the form of a feeling, a message or an impression. As time goes on, you will start understanding these communications. There may be occasions when these messages may be contaminated by one's subconscious urges, and thus it may be difficult to distinguish the true from the false. One point to remember is that supreme truth is harmony, and anything that aspires or leads towards that harmony and oneness is 'true' and anything that creates conflict is 'false'.

There may come a time in one's sadhana when one starts hearing the inner sound vibrations (*anahat nada*). At this stage, one can dispense with the repetition of the mantra, which is only used to still the conscious mind and body. When these sounds appear it is important to listen to the sounds in the right ear and to ignore those in the left. Sages in the past were possibly aware of the functions of the right hemisphere of the brain and therefore advised aspirants to listen to the sounds in the right ear. This would help the development of the intuitive and perceptive faculties with which the right hemisphere is associated. Then one should hear these sounds going down into the heart center and navel center successively and then into the centers below the navel. A point is reached when the whole body seems to vibrate with the sound. At this point it may be easy to understand that body is not just gross matter, but vibrant energy. If one could trace the movement of these energies in the body and regulate this harmonious movement through simple awareness, it would be helpful in promoting physical health and well-being.

To listen to this inner music, the mind and body must be in a proper receptive state as discussed above. A proper understanding of these inner vibrations helps a great deal in keeping the inward journey fast and smooth. These vibrations are as spiritual as any good music can be, and will bring about any changes necessary for the proper functioning of the body and mind. Again, much will depend upon the attitude of listening. In listening to the sounds with a serene and calm mind, without interpretation or qualification, the mind may go beyond these sounds.

If you are not using any mantra, but wish only to do a simple relaxed contemplation, try to feel with the entire being a sense of peace and harmony. In this state of peace and poise, imagination and feeling assume a power which is not known at the level of ordinary consciousness. While doing this relaxed contemplation, a most important thing to remember is that the mind should not be forced by will toward any particular point. Some schools advise fixing the attention between the eyebrows or the tip of the nose. The fixing of the eyes at these points generates stimuli in the optic nerves, which then produce sensations of different lights and colors. But this compulsive force of concentration produces a resistance in the mind which is undesirable. Therefore the eyes should be relaxed and kept still. If the eyes are closed, a good way to relax them is to imagine a blueish light in front of the eyes, which will automatically keep them motionless. Different lights may be experienced spontaneously, but since the value of these lights is not very great, there is no harm if some help is taken from the imagination.

This sadhana can be done by all, provided one understands that the communication so received is not from the highest reality or truth, but from the highest point of the unconscious mind or the world of sound. This is a journey into the psychic or intuitive plane — as opposed to the true spiritual plane, which lies beyond the mind, both conscious and unconscious. The advantage of this sadhana is that if we are in difficulty, faced with a problem which we cannot solve by ourselves, we can hand over the problem to this power after establishing communication with it. If we can feel that this power has taken charge of the problem, and hold this feeling in our mind, in due course of time we will be surprised at the efficiency and ease with which the problem is solved. There is no problem of life which cannot be thus solved. However, one word of warning is essential. We are walking in a very, very sacred domain — in the inner temple of our being. Let us touch everything with clean hands and mind. Let us not make a play of it, for the penalty for improper use of this power is very high.

It is hoped that after having experienced this beauty and power, one may realize that all wealth — external or internal — proceeds from this source which is within us. This realization may demolish the sense of greed and acquisitiveness from which we have suffered for so long. Insecurity and fear may completely disappear in life, because by now we have realized that fear and insecurity proceed from thought, which separates itself from this supreme power.

Having gone this far, and having seen the powers of the unconscious mind, we may feel disinterested in all these powers and, having turned our backs on them, we may take the final jump to discover the Supreme Reality which lies beyond the mind—both conscious and unconscious—which is the ultimate source of all powers in the universe.

While going through the different layers of the unconscious mind, it is well to remember that although one experience may follow another in chronological time, we should not build psychological time by measuring our progress and movement. There is no real movement as long as we are wandering in the maze of the unconscious mind. It is all within us. We may witness the highest peak today and tomorrow descend into a valley, and the next day begin an ascent once again. It is like a mountainous journey, with ups and downs, in mist and fog.

Perhaps the real spiritual journey begins when we are no longer interested in this vast panorama of the unconscious, with all its powers and siddhis. As a result of this tremendous discontent—and of the silence which arises out of the awareness of the limitation of all our efforts, processes and methods to transcend the boundaries of mind—an explosion takes place within us. We stop moving, and in this stillness, this silence, that Supreme Reality comes down to us. This is the beginning of the real spiritual journey.

The Human Mind
and Its Structure

The mind is essentially a storehouse of past memories and experiences, whether conscious or unconscious, individual or collective, from which thought springs. It is also full of all the instinctive fears and emotions inherited from its animal existence throughout the evolutionary process.

What characterizes the human mind? Is it not thought? Thought alone makes us cognizant that there is a mind. If there is no thought, there is no mind as we know it. Thought is a combination of words or symbols which spring up from memory. Memory is the past. Recent research* has shown that memory is chemical in nature; hence it is mechanical and material. Memory is also selective in nature and is based on the pleasure/pain principle. Whatever is pleasurable is cherished, protected and stored, and whatever is painful is suppressed and relegated to the unconscious layers. Hence memory is conditioned, as is the thought springing up from it. Thought—however modified, trimmed or expanded—always remains conditioned, old and mechanical.

Biologically, the structure of the whole of the human organism, including the brain, is adapted to the basic function of survival. All the unconscious reflexes of the body are directed towards the same goal. On the conscious level, when the process of learning begins, the emphasis starts to change from physical

*Dr. Georges Ungar at Houston's Baylor College of Medicine claims to have isolated a chemical which represents fear of darkness. (*Journal of the Indian Medical Association*, 2/16/71.)

survival to psychological survival. At this stage comes the cultivation of pleasure and the avoidance of pain. On the physical level, pleasure and pain perform a biologically protective function, but on the psychological level this cultivation leads to the formation and strengthening of a psychological center, the *I* or the *me*. This center is built up around the central core of the basic thought 'I'. It accumulates around itself all the conditioned reflexes which are based on psychological pleasure. At an early stage of development, these psychological pleasures begin to conflict with the physical well-being.

At the simplest level, learning and conditioning are integral processes; on the purely physical level learning implies conditioning. But at the psychological level, conditioning comes into conflict with learning. As conditioning strengthens, learning gradually comes to a stop and the human mind becomes fossilized. Then the mind is not only in conflict with the body but also with itself. Psychological pleasure is not an integral whole; one pleasure is in conflict with another and thus the mind is in conflict with itself. The structure of the human mind at present is based on conditioning. Conditioning tends to reinforce itself and form grooves, patterns of behavior which destroy freedom and true happiness. There is no inherent mechanism in the brain which can reverse the process of conditioning; a conditioned mind cannot decondition itself through a process or an effort. Conditioning can only break through a shock or an explosion. Such shocks are delivered by life in large numbers every day. If one does not escape psychologically from such situations but instead faces facts as they are, a tremendous amount of energy is generated which shatters conditioning and renews the mind. The brain and the body will continually renew themselves if psychological pleasures do not interfere.

Normally, thought is causing friction and conflict and reducing the energy of the brain; the brain cells are getting worn out and old. So in order to have a fresh and young mind which is highly energetic, we will have to find the significance and meaning of psychological thought, discover its mainspring, and see if it can come to an end. Secondly, we will have to discover if there is any other type of thought which will not interfere with the energy pattern of the silent meditating brain. If we go deeply into this question, we will find that both these possibilities are not merely hypotheses, but actually realizable states—and not at the end of a long tortuous process of practice and spiritual discipline, but immediately, in the present, the moment we are earnestly and energetically interested in this discovery.

It is clear that a fresh, energetic and empty mind is capable of seeing and understanding something new. Can it be possible otherwise? Can a mind tired and overwrought with conflicting thoughts, worries or agitation be capable of understanding and solving a new problem? Obviously not. So our immediate problem is to find out if thought can end, and also if it is possible to live an ordinary everyday life with a silent and energetic meditative mind. To live such active vigorous life, we will have to discover the kind of thought which is necessary for living and does not destroy the energy of the mind.

In proceeding further with this enquiry into the nature and meaning of thought, it will be of interest to note the changes in the electrical patterns of the brain as recorded by the electroencephalograph. There are four basic patterns, corresponding to four states of consciousness. The first state, in which there is complete mental and physical rest, is characterized by alpha waves which have a frequency of 8 to 13 cycles per second and a voltage of up to 50 microvolts. This is a state of relaxed contemplation, and is easily attained by closing the eyes or sitting in a dark or semi-dark room with the body in a still, relaxed position. This state is characterized subjectively by great peace, calm and exhilaration. It is perhaps the basic state of the human mind, from which either the state of wakefulness may proceed, characterized by intellectual or emotional activity on the one hand, or a state of deeper quietude merging into sleepiness and deep sleep on the other. As the mind moves into intellectual or emotional activity, the alpha waves are replaced by beta waves, with a frequency above 13 cycles per second and a reduced voltage of between 20 and 25 microvolts. Thought energy is thus characterized by high frequency but low voltage, which reflects an increase in resistance and conflict. On the other hand, when the quietude of the meditative state deepens, the frequency falls further, to between 4 and 8 cycles per second, and the voltage increases up to 100 or 150 microvolts (theta waves). In deep sleep or narcosis the frequency may fall to between 0.5 and 3.5 cycles per second and the voltage may increase up to 250 or 300 microvolts (delta waves). Sleep is a passive state, and an ordinary human mind, unaccustomed to mental silence, soon passes into sleep. However, as sensitivity and energy of the mind increase through meditation, the mind can stay in this state of deep silence easily. When the voltage is kept steadily high, a state is reached in which there is a possibility of a sparking or explosion taking place.

Many explosions are taking place in the human mind daily, and they can be divided into two main types. One takes place in the positive field of limited and narrow consciousness, in a small corner of the human mind. This is brought about by intense desire, emotion, drugs, or various methods of concentrating thought—or by lulling thought with rapid deep breathing accompanied by a background of music or wild chanting. Such explosions may lead to a great expansion of consciousness and a consequent sense of release, but since they occur in only a small segment of the human mind, ultimately they do not take the mind out of the shell of ego, and only act as palliatives or at best soothing escapes from sorrow. They will never solve the fundamental problem of the *I* and *me*.

The second type of explosion takes place in a silent meditative mind as described above—a negative field in which both conscious and unconscious minds come to naught. Or, while in a state of sorrow, if we can block all routes of escape such as verbalization, amusement, drink, drugs, or sex, we can face sorrow directly. If we do nothing about it but just live with it—feel it completely and intensely—then in this bottled-up negative energy of sorrow an explosion takes place. This is the greatest possible explosion of which the human mind is capable, in which there is a complete and irreversible transformation of sorrow or negative silence into a positive state of love and great beauty. This love is at the same time personal and impersonal, individual and universal; a new principle of integrated intelligence comes into being.

As in any explosion, waves are set up, and the individual mind is in communication with the whole of the universe. Thus changes taking place in the individual human mind influence the whole of the human race, even without verbal communication. This is the highest miracle of life, and a human being who has not discovered this state of consciousness is unfortunate indeed. Only when this is experienced does man become really free—not from any particular thing or event, but actually free of both outer and inner environment, inasmuch as he can face any situation in life adequately.

The Totally Silent Mind

To realize the truth as it is without any distortion, the mind must be completely emptied of its various urges, longings and fears. This cannot be brought about by compulsion or suppression but only by simple awareness, by looking at every thought or feeling as it is—without condemnation, approbation or justification. The censor must become quiet and passive if this watchfulness, which is unmotivated, is to operate. It is to be understood that awareness is not to be practised as a method to induce silence of the mind or to rid it completely of all thoughts. Such an attitude will only operate as condemnation, and resistance will immediately develop in the mind. The idea is just to look and see the stuff which comprises the mind. If we are interested in observing and discovering the facts as they are, we will soon find that the movement and succession of thoughts in the mind becomes very slow indeed. It is not sufficient to watch mechanically and see that one thought is succeeding another; we must watch each and every thought as it arises—see its content, cause and meaning at the same time. The aim is to understand each and every thought in its entirety. If this meditation is done earnestly and with interest, we will soon find the mind becoming silent—a natural state in which there is no conflict throughout the various layers. There may be certain mechanical memories or thoughts still operating, but even they do not interfere with this silence.

Out of this silence, we can look at different external objects or facts; or the mind can look at itself and experience a quality of peace and stillness. In this state there is no observer or observed, but only simple awareness of silence.

In the beginning, it may be advisable to sit in a chair or on the ground in a convenient and easy posture, with the spine, neck and head erect. There is no particular necessity to sit in *siddhasana* or *padmasana* (the lotus posture); these asanas can have definite psychosomatic benefits, but the less we depend on outer aids the better it will be in the long run. We should sit with a still body, with the eyes open or closed, whichever is convenient. A short session of deep rhythmic breathing will help in relaxing both the mind and body. As soon as we close our eyes we will find that the mind starts wandering hither and thither. Let us not force the mind, but just watch its various movements with love and care—as we would look at a flower. Some unpleasant thoughts may arise, but we must understand that it is our mind, it is what it is—and unless we can see the whole of ourself as it is, we will never be free and happy. Once we start looking in this way, suppressed experiences in the unconscious start unfolding themselves, so this observation not only generates tremendous energy but also unburdens the unconscious mind. We thus become aware of ourself, the whole of our conscious and unconscious mind, without inhibitions and distortions. This meditation will do what no amount of psychoanalysis can ever hope to achieve.

This is a journey without end, as is the movement of truth itself—ever unfolding, ever new, beyond the shackles of time and space. Once this state is discovered, many of the vexing problems of modern life will be solved easily. Perhaps with such an alert, energetic and intelligent mind no problem will be so great or difficult as to defy solution.

Upon the emergence of the intellect in human evolution, the emotions and other vital instincts of animal life were relegated to the background. In the same way, when the fragmented human mind—dominated by the intellect—becomes integrated, the intellect will be relegated to its proper place. It is only when this realization has come that the approaches of *jnana, bhakti* and *karma yoga,* as different possible means of approach to reality, will be seen to be absolutely inadequate. Any approach aiming to bring different fragments together one by one will never bring about integration; the total thus realized will still be fragmented.

How one can live happily in a complex modern world—without any psychological effort, without strife or conflict—will no longer be speculation or theory, but an actual, tangible reality, realizable now and here. This meditation—which is simply observing everything with full attention—will not be a discipline or ritual to be performed at certain set times of the day; it will be a way of life. It may be said that life will be meditation except when intense intellectual activity is undertaken. As soon as the mind is free of such activity, it will return to its original meditative state.

It is only now that two words—*philosophy* and *darshan*—will acquire meaning. *Philosophy* will no longer mean a speculative system, but love of truth. Similarly *darshan*—which is the equivalent of "philosophy" in Sanskrit, and literally means *to see* or *to look*—will be understood as it ought to be.

Life is a movement, a process without end. In this movement which we call life, there are moments when there is complete clarity, full understanding without a shadow of doubt or uncertainty. A moment later, when we become aware of this knowledge, newly gained wisdom and enlightenment, we realize that what we knew before as right was ignorance, and what we know now is the only truth. In this moment of being occupied with ourself, in trying to be definite and secure in our newly-gained knowledge, the current of life has moved miles ahead and we are once again in the backwaters. This is the beginning of confusion; the seed of ignorance is sown in this moment. If the mind, in its desire for self-satisfaction, becomes stupefied with the feeling of having become a realized soul—if people start worshipping us and we get surrounded by a host of well-meaning admirers—we are doomed to a life of continued illusion and self-deception. It is not that truth is not loving and kind, that it shall not knock at our doors again. But when we have become so great, sitting on such a high pedestal of name and fame, we have left truth no room, no space above us to enter; truth may only come to us through narrow chinks and crevices—from floor level—and chances are we will not see it.

It would be so much better if we did not entertain any ideas about truth nor about the source from which it can come. Let us not bind ourselves with the assumption that it can come from a guru highly erudite, learned and famous, from a particular sacred book, or even through worshipping an avatar or prophet, past or present. The danger is that if our yearning and belief are too intense, we will realize our idea of truth, but not truth—because truth is not an idea. Such a realization appears to be truth, but it is not—we merely see our original thought, idea or symbol, which was previously an abstraction, now concretized, more satisfying and stimulating. The conversion of one form of energy into another, or of energy into matter or vice versa, is a scientific fact which is taking place daily in laboratories all over the world. If this laboratory happens to be the human mind, it does not basically alter the scientific fact of energy conversion. If we can show that repetition of a mantra—production of certain sounds in a particular manner, coupled with intensity and concentration of thought—can produce material results, what we demonstrate is that thought can be converted into matter. It is not something new. The recent finding that memory, which is essentially organized thought, is chemical in nature, is a discovery which should dispel many superstitions based on preachings of so-called spiritual gurus, past or present, all over the world.

When the mind is hypnotized through a drug, suggestion or the repetition of a mantra or formula, it is possible to explore certain deeper layers of the unconscious mind, and find great stimulation and satisfaction from these so-called new experiences, sounds and visions. The experiences appear new because the sadhaka is becoming conscious of them for the first time—although if it is looked at with astute observation, it can be discovered that they are all from the reservoir of past memories, whether individual or collective. If the experience of the new is to take place, the mind must be totally free of the past, and none of these methods will do.

The other fallacy which is quite common in spiritual literature is the assumption that when we concentrate on a point or a thought, it starts progressively breaking into its finer and subtler fragments until the thought is completely negated. The noted tantric scholar Kaviraj Gopi Nath has developed this idea mathematically. In his system he defines a unit of psychological time as the time required to pronounce a letter of the alphabet. Through concentration, this unit of thought is broken up into smaller and subtler parts progressively, on through the different levels of the unconscious mind, until on the ninth plane it is divided into five hundred and twelve parts. Then $1/512$ becomes equivalent to zero for practical purposes—thought is presumed to have come to an end. No doubt the mind becomes very subtle, almost free of thought—inasmuch as the total identification of the observer with the observed will result in complete negation of the conflict. But the basic nature of the mind will remain as before.

Concepts, imagination, mantra and hypnotism have their own place in life: in healing the sick, in the development of intuitive and other paranormal faculties of mind, and in building up a comfortable material world. However, they are not only inadequate, but very dangerous when they are used for brainwashing the minds of simple people or as a means to discover ultimate reality or truth.

The Art of Observation

Observation involves three aspects: the observer, the observed, and the act of observation. When we look at an object, the rays of light travel from the object to the eyes and then through the optic nerve to the brain. There is always an interval, however small, between the perception of an object and its recognition or naming. Moreover, if we observe carefully—say while driving a car on a busy street—we are aware of the crowd, the other vehicles, and the street without consciously thinking about them; we see all these things but we do not think about them or name them. This first stage, prior to recognition and naming, is a state of non-verbal or thought-free perception (*nirvikalpa jnana* or pure perception). From this pure perception we proceed to thought, recognition and naming (*savikalpa jnana*). When the observer identifies the observed, it classifies and qualifies it. The observer identifies itself with the observed if it is pleasant and desirable, and alienates itself from the observed if it is unpleasant and undesirable. However, in the psychological field, these processes of identification and alienation are one and the same; one implies the other. In neither case is there an integration of the observer and the observed, and hence there is no observation, only distortion. The space between the observer and the observed, in which self-projection takes place, is psychological space.

When we come into intimate contact with an object—say we hold a spoon or a cup in our hand—we become aware of its texture, solidity and temperature. When this object is placed at a distance from us, we can think of these qualities but cannot feel them. This psychological space, in which we substitute thought for actual contact, is the space in which the observer alienates itself from the observed. To observe an object completely, to come into intimate contact with an object, it is necessary that this psychological space in which thought operates—or in other words, this psychological space which is nothing but thought about the object—must come to an end. When thought comes to an end, there is an intimate contact between the observer and the observed. This psychological fusion of the observer and the observed is true observation. In such a complete act of observation there is no observer in psychological form, though physically it still exists. Once the observer disappears, the separate psychological existence of the observed also comes to an end.

When this psychological distance remains, self-projection rather than observation takes place. In this space, the observer is constantly projecting its desires, aversions and knowledge, and so it is not seeing the observed, and hence not understanding what the observed actually is; it is only observing its own desires, aversions and knowledge. Furthermore, the moment recognition takes place and naming begins, further observation comes to an end, and the space between the observer and the observed reappears once again.

Therefore to observe anything correctly and to understand it, the observer must become silent and passive. This implies that the censor in the observer must come to an end. The observer must learn to be a silent witness, not only of the things outside itself but of its own inner movement as well—its thoughts, likes and dislikes. As one proceeds deeper with this kind of observation, the observer becomes silent and disappears; only the observed remains.

The observed is maintained as a separate entity only by the action of the observer; once the observer disappears, only pure observation remains. In other words, the ending of the observer and observed as separate entities, or their fusion, leads to simple, pure observation. In the act of observation, when the observer and the observed are fused, the mind undergoes a transformation; it becomes rich and full.

> *"Drastri drishyoparaktam chittam sar-*
> *vartham."*
>
> —Patanjali; IV:23

> *"A mind dyed with the fusion of the ob-*
> *server and the observed is full of all riches."*

It is to be seen that such observation is the only true observation, and that when there is a gap, space, or interval between the observer and the observed, self-projection takes place and distortion results. This self-projection is the destructive action of the ego, which destroys love and understanding and breeds endless strife and conflict. We know that the ego is the main source of violence, pain and sorrow. Innumerable methods have been devised since time immemorial to root out his ego, to annihilate this self, but pursuit of these methods has only pushed the ego deeper and deeper, and made it more and more subtle to the point of being unrecognizable. Man thought that he had solved the problem of the ego, but he could not escape being confronted by it, thriving and kicking at a different level. But if one can learn this art of observation, the problem of the ego can be solved once and for all.

> *"Visheshadarshina atma bhava bhava-*
> *narinivrittih."*
>
> —Patanjali; IV:25

> *"In one who truly sees (with this art of*
> *pure observation), ego (or selfhood) disap-*
> *pears."*

It is with this awareness, this simple and pure observation, that confusion and sorrow disappear. This correct understanding of one's relation to persons, things and ideas is the only basis for a new consciousness—one which unites humanity in a bond of love and eliminates sorrow, strife, and suffering. It is not in the invention of new sects and systems—which will only divide humanity as they have always done in the past—but rather in learning this art of observation, that salvation or freedom lies. Such freedom is possible for most people if they are serious about solving the problems of their lives.

Now some more energetic and courageous people can go a stage further, and transcend both awareness and understanding. This however cannot be understood intellectually, as the very thought or imagination of such a state is frightening. When awareness and understanding also disappear, what becomes of the human mind? Does it not become dead or inert? Does it not enter a state of great void *(maha shunya)* which is so frightening as to be worse than death? If one can look calmly, without the fear which imagination engenders, one can easily understand that awareness is needed only when one is in pain or sorrow, or when one is busy in some physical or intellectual activity. When one is not so occupied, what then is the need of awareness? Why cannot understanding take leave and go to rest? What then remains?

> *"Prasankhyaneypya kusidasya sarvatha*
> *vivekakhyate dharmamegha samadhi."*
>
> —Patanjali; IV:29

> *"One who is disinterested even in under-*
> *standing goes to a state of being beyond*
> *experiencing—the highest samadhi in which*
> *one is enveloped in one's innate nature*
> *(swabhav or dharma) like a huge cloud."*

The courage to go beyond awareness culminates in a state

beyond pleasure and pain, understanding and ignorance, in which awareness will only operate for short periods if necessary; for example, when attending to one's physical needs. This is a state which is apparently negative but which is full of active energy. In this state of highest truth, both negative and positive are not only completely blended, but fused into one.

How is one going to achieve this state? What practice, process or sadhana can help us to arrive at this point of the highest truth? Can we look to the past history of spirituality for an answer?

We can look at the Sankhya philosophy, whose followers from its very inception practised disinterested and passive awareness with the resultant complete cleavage between the observer and the observed. This practice led to a free play of unregenerate nature of four types, described by the Hindu books of wisdom as *bata* (childlike), *gadg* (dull, inert), *umat* (mad), and *pishacha* (unbalanced, ghostlike). These states occurred when the ego or the observer, through practice, became detached from this nature and no longer exercised control. The mind could be freed of conflict but could not be transformed. Perhaps Buddha, in his supreme moment of enlightenment, could break the circle of cause and effect and come upon that blessing, that light which is compassion for all beings. But what was the cause which preceded this effect, this enlightenment? Was it some method or some sadhana which Buddha had been practising for some time, or was it the ending of all methods by realizing their futility—and giving up any and every hope whatsoever? Perhaps it was a sense of total defeat and surrender which climaxed in this enlightenment. Could it be propagated further? And how many of Buddha's disciples in their turn received this enlightenment? This very interesting question has been beautifully discussed by Hermann Hesse in his novel "Siddhartha".

As with the Sankhyas, the way taught by Buddha, or perhaps by his followers, resulted in a certain sense of freedom, maintained by a constant practice of awareness. However, there was always an underlying subtle tension, in no way akin to spontaneous freedom and creative reality.

Lord Mahavira, the founder of Jainism, roamed in the forest in search of this spontaneous freedom. For twelve years he roamed and this freedom eluded him, and one day when he was tired and dismayed, devoid of any hope, there came this spontaneous freedom, this enlightenment, uninvited. After this enlightenment, everything changed—including his language, which was now intelligible to very few. His chief disciple, Gautama Muni, could understand him, but freedom did not come to him, though many others who listened to Gautama Muni attained salvation. Gautama Muni's freedom only came after the death of Lord Mahavira—that is, after the ending of Gautama Muni's last attachment, hope and refuge.

Then came Adishankara, the founder of Advaita or nondualistic philosophy, who taught meditation on the Maha Vakyas as 'Thou art that' and 'I am that'. The result was a state of self-hypnosis through incessant practice.

In recent times, the great sage Ramana Maharshi advised his followers against hypnotizing themselves with such formulas as 'I am that' or 'I am the Brahman', and insisted on making an enquiry, an incessant questioning into the nature of the self. With this approach, the result might have been far-reaching and deep—a great breakthrough of the shell of ego was indeed achieved—but some limitation did creep in, the limitation common to any method or system. The first flash of enlightenment that results is perhaps spontaneous, but by trying to maintain this state of nonduality through a conscious enquiry—by tiring out the intellect—a limitation is imposed on that state. After some practice, that state may appear to become spontaneous and natural, but it is no longer true spontaneity. In the same way, the identification of one's self with any so-called spiritual state puts a limitation on one's spiritual journey.

In modern times, Shri J. Krishnamurti has contributed immensely to the understanding of self. Many of those who listen to him attentively reach a state of silence. To an ordinary human mind, accustomed to positive replies or conclusions, this silence is boring and meaningless. This silence may be a real blessing and perhaps become a launching pad on the journey into a new dimension, but many people get disappointed and turn back. The importance of the role of Shri J. Krishnamurti is to be assessed not by the number of people who appreciate him or get disappointed, but by the refreshingly new approach and direction that he has given to this enormous question of self-knowledge.

Returning to the original question, from which we digressed: how are we to learn this art of observation? The relentless and earnest pursuit of this question is in itself meditation. The question is a difficult one and, as has been pointed out above, cannot be answered satisfactorily by anyone. The only way which can avail is to have an earnest desire to learn, and a relationship of love and affection between the observer and the observed. In this love all things are possible.

To sum up, it can be said that there are, broadly speaking, two ways of looking at a thing—for instance, a flower. One way is to look at a flower as a scientist, with the technical knowledge of the botanist or the herbalist. The second way is to look at it as would an artist or poet—with full attention and care, letting the flower make its total impact on the human mind. This total impact is received only when the observer is totally one with the flower.

So to learn this art of observation, we must have the seriousness and earnestness of a scientist and the sensitivity of a poet and artist. We may start by learning to observe a natural object such as a flower or a tree, because such objects do not evoke very strong emotional responses. As one goes on learning this art, one may proceed to look at things and persons which evoke strong emotional responses of liking and disliking. At this stage one looks at an object not only outside, but also inwardly—at one's own disturbances of anger, hatred or attachment. In such an observation, when one becomes fused with one's own anger and hatred, one learns the supreme art of transforming one's own basic nature— and at the same time one becomes free of both outer and inner environment.

Love

In examining the act of observation, we noticed that whenever a silent mind looks at a person or an object, the distance between the observer and the observed disappears. This state, in which the observer (the ego) comes to an end and fuses with the observed, is love. A youth may have looked at the face of a maiden many times in the past, but there comes a moment when he looks at her and for the first time discovers an overwhelming beauty—a beauty incomparable. There is a spontaneous sense of great awe and reverence for that beauty; nothing appears to be more beautiful. This state may last for a few moments or longer, depending on the background of the mind. In this state there is no desire or assertion, because the entity, the ego from which desires spring, is absent. There is no self-seeking or possessiveness, but rather an immense self-giving. Later on, when attachment and possessiveness enter, the sublime state of love is obscured and only a dead memory remains, which can be a cause of endless pain and sorrow. The human mind, in its present state of greed, ambition and violence, is incapable of living in this state of love for any length of time. However, it is capable of fabricating great philosophy and poetry around this central pillar, this experience which is so highly elusive and evanescent.

What is the source of this great sense of beauty? Is it the face of the beloved? The youth has seen this face a number of times before, but he never saw that beauty in it. He may become familiar with this face, he may possess this maiden as a wife, but then the chances are that in a few days the same face is no longer attractive and there comes a sense of boredom in which other faces start looking more beautiful. What has happened? In that supreme state of love, this beauty was incomparable, no other was more beautiful. Does it not mean that that beauty was not in the face of the beloved? Was it in the eyes of the lover, or was it something immense and supreme, transcending both the lover and the beloved?

Is this beauty personal or impersonal? Is it only the face of the beloved which is beautiful? Do not the trees, the flowers, the stars and the moon look beautiful in that state? Obviously that supreme love or beauty is both personal and impersonal at the same time. The dividing line between the divine and the human, the transcendent and the immanent disappears.

Can the human mind create this love and beauty, or is it only a spontaneous happening which sometimes blesses us? Having had a fleeting glimpse of it, the human mind has tried various methods to resurrect and recreate it. Man has tried to work up emotion to the highest pitch through aspiration, self-giving or identification. The path of *bhakti* or devotion is one such approach. As is common to any mental process, it consists of various levels and grades. There is the lower form *(aparabhakti)* in which the devotee and the adored have a separate existence; this is a relationship of duality. In the highest form *(parabhakti),* there is a complete identification of the devotee and the adored; we may say that there is only one existence in which the adored does not exist separately. This state of *parabhakti* very closely approximates the spontaneous love and beauty discussed above. It is similar, but not exactly the same, because in this state of devotion some admixture of thought energy always persists as an impurity.

Furthermore it must be clearly understood that such a single-minded devotion requires a very simple and innocent mind, like that of a Tulsidas, Soor Das or Mirabei: a mind which is a rare occurrence in this complex intellectual world, in these days of disbelief and lack of faith.

Moreover, the division between divine love and human, between spiritual and profane always remains. It is one thing to see the divine in a human being, and love that person as a manifestation of the divine; it is quite another to be in a state of love in which the divine and non-divine simply do not exist.

With great sincerity and single-minded aspiration—as advocated by Shri Aurobindo in his "Integral Yoga"—it is possible to reach a summit of divine love, a great power and blessing for the human mind. But any result which depends on human effort, howsoever subtle, is not really spontaneous, although it may appear so. Whatever is not spontaneous is not true love. In this yoga, we realize the highest conceptual divine love which has the semblance of reality, but it is not reality.

Now we are faced with a serious problem. We have seen one ennobling event, one truly transforming happening: this spontaneous love. We have also seen that the human mind, whatever it may do, however hard it may try, is incapable of capturing this beautiful state. What are we to do then? We can do nothing except realize the need for this great transforming principle in our lives. We must realize that we are incapable of doing anything to come upon this creative state—other than learning to surrender to our helplessness and be quiet. In this spontaneous silence, it is possible that we may be blessed by this great energy which we call love.

This state of love is not something completely foreign to the human mind. There must be a large number of people in the world whose lives have been blessed at one time or another by this great mysterious energy. But when it could not be understood, it could not become a steady flame and light; it became obscured and vanished. What is important is not only to come across this energy or merely touch it, but to prepare the mind through deep meditation to receive it; to remain in a state of active passivity so that this energy can stay undisturbed, a steady flame which completely transforms human life.

It is therefore necessary to understand the factors which obscure this light, as well as what can coexist with this energy without falsifying or distorting it. The mind must be simple and innocent—and if it is not so naturally or inherently, then it must become simple through the understanding of the destructive activities of the ego, its pursuit of the pleasures of name, fame and wealth. Only a mind which is free of greed, ambition and violence is capable of loving. But for this a complete reversal of the habitual pursuits of the mind is needed. Not only must the mind not pursue outer wealth, but it must bid goodbye to the accumulated inner wealth of memory and organized experience. Therefore it must also bid goodbye to arrogance, and so come to a state of complete humility.

Another important point that must be raised is the relation of sex and marriage to this state of love. Marriage as a relationship of two hearts in love is understandable; but marriage as a ritual with a social code and social obligations—which takes many things for granted and is based on the principles of attachment and possession—is quite contrary to the spirit of this spontaneous state. This possessiveness, with its consequent attachment, jealousy and hatred, is sure to destroy a beautiful relationship. But if two persons stay together in a state of complete freedom and mutual understanding, in such a relationship sexual relations need not be excluded. Sexual relations may or may not be there; the emphasis is not on sex but on love and understanding. Only when sex becomes the all-important, dominant factor is the relationship of love distorted and destroyed.

If there is a moderate sex impulse, which is not too strong and violent, and does not insist upon its own satisfaction to the exclusion of all other considerations, sex can be a compatible and harmonious blending, a crowning physical manifestation of the togetherness of a spiritual state. But for sex to be elevated to such a height, it must come as a spontaneous outflowing between two persons living in a relationship of love. Such an act cannot be pursued as a sensation or a pleasure, to which the ordinary human mind is so accustomed; this seeking is full of violence. An integral sexual relationship, free from violence and conflict, will not lead to any waste of energy. In such a relationship the problem of sex will be solved forever; and man will neither pursue sex as an escape nor will he try to overcome his sexual impulse. It is only when there is love in one's heart that sex can be understood.

In recent times, especially amongst the young, there has been a demand for free sex and free love. Love in its essence is always free, and without freedom love cannot be. But the slogan of free sex has become a new means of escape from boredom and may only ultimately bring frustration and sorrow. As has been mentioned earlier, sex is the one human activity in which there is a possibility of complete self-abandon and self-dissolution, however transient. This self-dissolution is only possible when the sexual relationship is approached in a state of great calm and mental silence, and not as a pursuit of a sensation or pleasure based on past memories. But for most people pursuing it as a pleasure or as an escape, sex is bound to be a very frustrating experience, for repeated seeking of a pleasure leads only to frustration and boredom. If we could manage it, we would seek new partners so as to have some newness in our experience, but after some time even this repeated search for new partners ends in boredom, conflict and frustration.

We may occasionally experience an egoless state in a sexual relationship, but from that evanescent feeling a state of superconsciousness or love cannot be built up. We may turn to sex in search of this state, but in doing so we are likely to go into a state of mechanical repetition. We can make use of thought energy by concentrating at a point away from the sexual act—building up the pleasure of concentration and transferring to it the pleasure of sex—but the sexual act is still likely to become mechanical. Substituting one pleasure for another is a poor way to understand sex and its complexities.

The only way is to discover love or superconsciousness in its own right, and once this light is touched, the same light may be used to illuminate the dark valley of sex and understand it. There is only one possible direction, and that is from superconsciousness

to sex, from love to sex. There is no way from sex to superconsciousness or love. Sex as a means of self-gratification and escape
must come to an end for love to be. Love is integral, and sex is only
a fragment of it. Sex can exist in love, but love cannot exist when
sex is exclusively pursued.

The beginning of love is the ending of meditation. When we
have love in our hearts, the intellect becomes silent and no longer
asks questions about God, the soul, or life hereafter; such questions appear irrelevant. It is only an unhappy mind which asks so
many sterile and useless questions. If we are in a state of love,
meditation becomes a burden, questions become a burden—all
that we need is to be silent in that spontaneous state. If we learn
not to act upon the mechanical urges of the intellect or desires of
the vital mind, but to live in such a way that things happen to us
instead of our planning them or bringing them about by an intellectual effort of will, a true transformation has taken place. This
transformation first takes place in the mind and is then gradually
reflected in the body. We do not perform miracles, but miracles
start happening in our lives.

The Art of Listening

Our contact with the external world is through the five senses. Out of these five, the most important are seeing and hearing, and in descending order of importance come taste, touch and smell. We have seen how distortion in observation takes place and how it may be corrected. Now we must carefully examine the factors which distort listening.

The moment we hear a word, we interpret and translate it into a synonym in order to understand it. Words relating to the physical or material world do not create much problem: words such as house, railway station, or train. But when we come to words which have a psychological import—such as nation, wife, prestige, God, soul or love—the situation at once changes and we respond differently. In most cases when the words "I", "my" and "mine" are added to any word, or if these words are implied indirectly, the situation becomes difficult and complicated. The human mind at once loses its equanimity and responds with resistance or identification, and psychological pleasure and pain come into operation. This disturbance distorts listening. Superficial responses of memory manifest, which prevent any word from going to the depths of the human mind. This resistance creates a chain reaction and ultimately destroys peace and freedom.

All of us enjoy listening to a talk which is pleasant, stimulating and entertaining. What does such a talk do to us? When it is in conformity with our beliefs, such a talk only fortifies the prison walls of our conditioning. When we listen to a talk pertaining to a

60

book or to some other person, we either isolate ourselves from it or identify with it, depending upon our displeasure or pleasure. We can easily approve or condemn such persons or books or feel a great satisfaction at having learned something new. But what have we learned? We have only exercised our conclusions based on our conditioning once again.

A talk which does not conform to the pattern of our conditioning becomes unpleasant and disturbing, and we react very strongly. But perhaps it is only such a talk which can lay bare the hidden complexes, the animal passions, and the whole ugliness of our mind. If we could listen to such a talk with a peaceful and quiet mind—without interpreting or qualifying such words, without reacting from the superficial layers of our mind—a great transformation could be brought about in the human mind. But is it possible to listen in such a way? I think if the deep importance of such listening is very clearly understood, one can easily learn not to give in to superficial reactions. As each word is listened to patiently and quietly, as each word goes deeper and deeper, the reaction produced may be watched, felt, and absorbed completely; in this way the mind is transformed.

It is often said that we should listen to words without translating or interpreting them. One may ask if this is at all possible. When we listen to a word it produces an automatic reaction. We should watch and feel this reaction with our whole being, patiently and effortlessly, and not interpret this automatic reaction into another set of words or symbols. Such an interpretation or translation keeps us at a very superficial level, and although we think that we have understood the word, in actual fact all understanding is destroyed.

Real listening implies a direct perception, without any images about ourselves or the speaker intervening. If we can be in such a state of complete attention, and absorb the whole impact of what we hear, all images and conditionings are shattered; the mind is rejuvenated, made innocent and fresh to learn and live an eternal life. To learn to listen to everything without and within with complete attention is the greatest discipline or *tapasya* of which the human mind is capable. The reward is rich beyond description. It is often stated that the supreme truth or reality cannot be communicated by speech; but if one learns the art of listening, one can find that God or absolute reality speaks from each and every center or particle in the universe. Then one need not go to great teachers and masters for learning; one will find songs in books and sermons in stones.

Prolonged sitting in meditation, doing *japa*, concentration, or chanting a mantra, may all bring about a hypnotic trance and a sense of great release; but true wisdom will forever remain a dream. The two arts of observation and listening will bring about a tremendous understanding, not only of the self, but of the whole world.

Time: Physical and Psychological

While studying the act of observation in the preceding pages, we were indirectly studying the meaning of psychological space, for life moves on the twin wheels of time and space. To understand life, one will have to understand the meaning and significance of these two terms.

Physical time and space do not create much problem for man. He is on the road to mastery of this space and time, and in this race he is proceeding very quickly. However, apart from physical time and space, man is always creating psychological time and space. He imprisons himself in this psychological time and space and destroys his freedom.

Physical time proceeds in a chronological order, an orderly succession of events: night follows day and day follows night, Monday follows Sunday and Tuesday follows Monday in a fixed, systematic order. But when we come to psychological time, which is thought based on memory, do we think in a systematic order from yesterday to today and from today to tomorrow? Do we not sometimes think forward and then a moment later backward into the past again? In physical time, we can only proceed forwards, we cannot go backwards. What is gone is gone; the past is dead. But with psychological time this is not so. Psychological time is essentially past, as it is based on memory and thought. This past never dies—psychological time continually revives it. There is a constant movement, from present to future and from future to past in quick succession. This chaotic movement of psychological time is a source of conflict, misery and sorrow. The aim of meditation is to be free of this psychological time and space; indeed we may say that the understanding of this time and space is meditation.

We have seen that the space between the observer and the observed, the interval which separates the two, is the field in which self-projection and the ego flourish and grow. True observation, in which the observer and the observed become one, is the ending of this space, and the beginning of understanding, freedom, and love.

In the same way, if we look at time, we see that we exist in the present, but when we think, we think either of the past or the future, for there is no thought in the present. Our thought about the future is based on the experiences of the past, and therefore it is actually only modified past; if we had no past, there would be no thought about the future. Thought moves from the past to the present and from the present to the future, like the movement of a pendulum to and fro, without resting for even a moment in the present. Simply stated, this means that thought, which is the past or the future, alienates itself from existence, which is only in the present. We may live for a hundred years, but our actual life—the actual existence of which we become intimately aware at any given moment—is the now, the present. We may think of tomorrow, but when tomorrow arrives we become aware of it only as today, not as tomorrow. Life is only now; yesterday and tomorrow are thought and imagination.

Therefore to understand life and truly enjoy it, to observe and look at it, we have to give our whole attention to it today, now, in the present moment. In modern times we talk a great deal about the need to live in the present, but to live from moment to moment implies a quick and peaceful mind, a mind free of greed and ambition, and at the same time rich and full of energy. Such a mind is the result only of very deep and profound meditation. If we are running after name, fame, money or power, we have hardly any time to observe life or to discover its richness and depth. And unless we observe life, we will always be running after outer riches and power. Each step that we take in that direction impoverishes our life more and more. If we look at life superficially and casually, we will only be aware of a great hollowness and boredom. We try to fill this void or hollowness with superficial sensory pleasures or outer riches, and yet this void always remains as fathomless as before. If we are to transcend this void, this boredom, we must look at it, feel it completely, and not run away from it. When the void becomes the observed and the observer, the *I* can completely integrate itself with the observed, the void undergoes a transformation which unfolds the richness and depth of life. With that energy and attention, we can live from moment to moment, we can live in the present. Does it imply that we will not think at all, that no thought will flit across our mind? Perhaps some thoughts which are essential to physical existence will occur—we may have to put aside some money, food and clothing for the needs of tomorrow—but beyond such bare necessities we will not pursue money, power or fame to enrich ourselves or to build prestige.

To come to this simplicity and this understanding, we will have to understand psychological time again and again in its various manifestations — as thought which springs from the past to the future; as the future in which we think we will find our security and happiness; as the past in which we had some very sweet and rich experiences; as death which will come to us in the near or distant future. This thought process operates in psychological time, not in physical time which is the present. If we meditate on time we can easily see that the smallest unit of time is a moment. Moment succeeds moment, and this succession of moments goes on endlessly in an eternal procession. The life and existence which we can palpably feel, experience, and enjoy at any given time, has meaning and significance only for a moment, for this smallest unit of time. And if we can understand the significance of a moment, we will see that in its womb a moment holds eternity, holds the secret of life, death, joy and sorrow. At any given moment there is no thought, no fear, no death; there is no pleasure, no pain, no experience. The mind is silent and still, free of all thought. Existence and thought are fused into a whole. Mind and life are a totality in which there is no cleavage, no space and hence no time. In a moment we see both time and the negation of time. A moment is eternity and beyond eternity; one who understands a moment understands everything.

Without following these lines attentively, one may feel these words to be the outcome of a poetic imagination, but if we look for ourselves we will find the truth of these statements. Let us think of a moment. In this brief unit of time can we think of anything? Any thought will occupy more than a moment. At this moment let us look at our surroundings with full attention, and also look within to see if we can entertain any thought or idea in this brief span. Perhaps now the moment is over. In the succeeding moment let us do it all over again. What is the result? Is it different or the same? The mind is still and calm, and life is moving from moment to moment. Is there any boredom in this moment? Is there any joy in this moment? If there is, we are not aware of it. Are we aware of anything in this one moment? Perhaps awareness has also gone to sleep. What are we left with? We do not know. Are we ignorant or wise? We do not know. But we are living and active, we are not sleeping or dead. This is the beauty of existence, which is touched neither by thought nor by awareness. This is the beauty and richness of life which is revealed in a moment. Let us not make it a game of moment-chasing. It is possible that in the next moment we may lose all this joy; loss of attention may dissolve this newly discovered light and freedom. But if we again meditate on a moment, become aware of that actual existence of life only as a moment, then we come once again upon that fragrance and beauty which is born out of understanding.

> *"Kshanatatkramayo sanyamad vivekajam jnanam."*
> —Patanjali; III: 53

> *"Meditation on a moment and on the succession of moments brings enlightenment."*

Awareness and Understanding

By this time let us hope that we are well on our way in discovering the art of observation. We have been watching our thoughts, ideas, emotions and responses in action, in life. We have meditated on time: on time as a moment, time as thought, time as ego, and time as death. During all this we have become progressively aware of many intricate and devious movements of mind. This progressive awareness has added a new dimension to our understanding. Sometimes we lose the thread of awareness and suffer as a consequence. How many times have we not thought of practising awareness assiduously and constantly so that sorrow and suffering may not touch us? But should we give in to this temptation? The practice of anything—except on the physical level where it may be a necessity—will give a semblance of joy and freedom; but actually is it not bound to fix our mind, ourself, at a particular static level and deny all movement—the movement so essential to the discovery of new vistas and the highest summit? A mind which begins its journey without self-projections or preconceived notions about the goal and aim—a mind which moves with an insatiable discontent—goes fastest and highest.

As we go deeper and deeper, the mind becomes richer and richer. It seeks and depends less and less upon such outer pleasures as name, fame and sex. The dawning of awareness brought forth a flame, a light which marked the first lap of our journey from darkness to light—from ignorance to understanding and self-knowledge. Progressively we may feel that this awareness, this understanding, is becoming a new fetter, a new chain and a burden. If we are not bent upon building up our prestige or ego on the pedestal of name and fame—which may be provided by this newly awakened knowledge—we are at the last door which opens into the great silence *(maha shunya)*. Here knowledge and understanding go to sleep. Here the gap between pleasure and pain, sorrow and joy becomes so small and insignificant that we feel only a movement—a ripple so soft and gentle—between positive and negative, between *Shiva* and *Shakti*. Nothing remains but a state of indescribable joyless joy.

The Guru

Who is the guru? Is the guru personal or impersonal? Is the guru essential for spiritual progress? It appears necessary to examine these very pertinent questions.

Reality or truth cannot be divorced from the total life process. If there is any truth, God or reality, it must be discovered in the very temple of life. Any God divorced from this life only leads to antagonism and contradiction. Any such God, if existing at all somewhere, can at best be a fragment of this whole which we call life. Life is constantly teaching us by shifting its scenes in a rapid succession of events; there could be no greater guru than this. And of course this initiation may come from a plant, a flower, an animal, a bird or a book.

This light may also come from a person, and it may be necessary for many persons to take initiation from a human guru. For simple people, innocent of mind, sensitive of spirit and in communion with nature, perhaps no human guru is necessary, because they have an open perception and are able to learn from every source. But for people who are not so sensitive, it may be necessary to take initiation from a human guru. If such recourse has to be taken, then the following points may be laid down as guidelines.

A real guru is one who teaches his disciple how to think, and not what to think. One who awakens intelligence in the disciple is the real guru. He is like a teacher in a post-graduate class, guiding and bringing forth a true spirit of enquiry, helping the student to explore rather than giving him some ready-made dogmas or creeds—however high or noble. Such a teacher must have humility, simplicity of heart, and a love of truth if he is to inculcate the same in the disciple. He must be able to communicate with the disciple on the same level. If on the other hand he acts as an authority—which by its very nature thwarts enquiry and learning—such a person is not a true guru at all. If he is ambitious, desirous of name and fame or wealth, he cannot have a really affectionate and loving relationship with the disciple. He will be incapable of communicating that state which we call love. A person who desires to be worshipped or even encourages others to worship him, overtly or covertly, is incapable of being a real teacher. An aspirant struggling to become free of ignorance may be in need of a teacher, but he should avoid a guru who is in search of disciples. Only one who is free and loves freedom will be able to inculcate the love of freedom in others.

If one has a guru who does not embrace humility, he must beware, for then he is in the hands of a living God—and a living God can be very terrible and tyrannical. Thanks to the growth of democracy and freedom, the possibilities of living Gods assuming absolute control over a large number of human beings is receding. Nevertheless, serious people must beware of falling prey to the magic of the mass media, of publicity and propaganda, and must always remember that what seems to be very comforting, assuring and secure can become the greatest bondage—a fetter from which there may be no escape.

If we cannot find a real guru—and such persons in the present world are very few indeed—it is far better to be without any guru and face life alone as best as we can. If we are honest with ourselves, and clear in our motives, nature will never let us down.

In the Upanishadic period in India, the guru, to awaken intelligence in the disciple, would always lead him to discover truth for himself by encouraging a spirit of enquiry in him. It was only much later, when the spirit of enquiry was replaced by an extreme desire for security, that the teacher assumed authority, as did the despotic king and the priest. Let us hope that we are now at the dawn of a new age, when old values and patterns are dying fast. A new spirit of revolt, a new era of incessant questioning, is coming of age, and whatever is false is likely to crumble like a house of cards.

The teacher of the new age will be a functionary, along with other functionaries serving at various levels in the new social order. However, these functionaries will not exploit their positions to build status. For a man who realizes truth, freedom is very sacred—his own as well as that of others. The very beauty of freedom is that it is indivisible.

Even if the teacher does not build up authority, the disciple may unconsciously build up the authority of the teacher for his own psychological satisfaction and security. This can hardly be otherwise, unless the disciple from the outset also learns to cherish freedom more than anything else. But as long as the disciple is attached to any pleasure, he always has some guru, some authority; his own pleasure acts as his guide and guru. Realizing all this, one may go beyond the necessity of an outer guru; but what about the inner guru, the authority of one's own experience?

In the first stage of the journey, it was necessary to have one's own first-hand experience and not to depend on another person's experience. But after having had so much experience, it is time to realize that all experience, whether others' or one's own, is incapable of measuring the fathomless ocean of life. Absolute truth lies beyond the pale of all experience. So when the authority of our own experience goes, what are we left with? We are so light, empty and free of all burden; and with this emptiness, this innocence, we are on the threshold of non-experience—the highest peak of realization from which everything proceeds and develops, the negative fountainhead of all life.

It is just possible that this book may have provided an initial impetus to some, or helped them occasionally on their journey. But now, if they can come to a point where they need no book, no person to depend upon in their journey of life, blessed will be that moment. For the last lap of the journey, whether in this phenomenal world or on the highest plane of spirituality, is to be made alone. The gate is so narrow that two cannot pass through at the same time.

"Strait is the gate and narrow is the way which leadeth unto life."

—New Testament; Matthew 7:14

Diet and Health

The role of food in the adult body is to replace worn-out tissues and maintain the body weight. However, food alone is not sufficient to bring about an energetic state of the body; mental and physical alertness depend predominantly on psychological factors. If food alone were sufficient to sustain a high level of energy, there would be no need for stimulants such as tea, coffee, alcohol, etc., to which most people are addicted. If a person develops a peaceful and meditative mind, his physical needs for food and sleep are liable to change. The amount of food previously taken may become excessive, and cause overweight, lethargy and disease. If psychological dependence on food can be eliminated, the body learns to adjust itself to a reduced food intake, and a high degree of physical and mental alertness can be maintained. Such an interaction of mind and body is normal and conducive to an integrated life, but the development of spiritual or psychological states—on the basis of fasting or semi-starvation, hatha yoga, drugs or self-hypnosis—is not desirable. Such induced states cannot bring about an integrated personality, because of their fragmentary nature.

An important question, asked invariably by all aspirants, is about the type of food which is compatible with a spiritual life. Too much conditioning in the mind about food, as in any other direction, is undesirable. Food should obviously be sufficient and wholesome, but on what criterion? The science of nutrition is still in its infancy; much research remains to be conducted to determine food's positive effects upon health, the hazards of excess, and the basis of unusual responses to, or demands for, specific foods. Under such circumstances, blind acceptance of the modern nutritionists' one-sided approach is unscientific and dangerous.

Civilized man has developed so many tastes and habits, and these are not always conducive to healthy living. Taste buds are provided by nature so that the organism can select proper foods and avoid harmful ones; but man, using his intellect—or rather misusing his intellect—has taken to using excessive amounts of salt, sugar and condiments to stimulate his appetite. Thus he has blunted his capacity to experience natural hunger and taste, thereby opening the flood-gates to excessive eating of improper foods. Most of the diseases of modern civilization are due to over-eating and to improper food.

In recent times, there has been a call to go back to nature, perhaps in disregard of the nutritionists' warnings. But there is evidence to suggest that men and animals have an inherent physiological mechanism which guides them to choose a nutritious diet, provided that the selection is not too narrowly limited by other factors. Presumably we learn to associate certain foods with a sense of bodily improvement.*

It is a common observation that a dog eats grass in preference to normal food when suffering from constipation. This is an example of what the yogis term consciousness of the body. This consciousness has been dulled or nearly destroyed in civilized man by the development of various notions, habits, addictions and superficial pleasures. This in turn creates conflict between the natural pleasures of a sound and healthy body, and the artificially created pleasures which destroy bodily health. This consciousness of the body must be rediscovered if man is to lead an integrated life, full of joy and happiness.

As the mind becomes more sensitive and energetic, one usu-

*Wright & Samson: Applied Physiology, 10th edition, p. 445.

ally finds that external stimulants to whip up the body and mind are unnecessary. The need for excessive food, highly seasoned food, and animal food becomes less and less.

Bodily growth comes to an end between the ages of twenty to twenty-five years. After this age span, slow degenerative changes start taking place, such as arteriosclerosis—hardening of the arterial walls which is hastened by a high-caloric, high-fat and high-protein diet. The following guidelines, in combination with adequate exercise and deep breathing, may be found helpful in maintaining the body, while at the same time slowing down these degenerative changes.

1. It must be clearly understood that food is meant only to compensate for wear and tear on the body; the immediate source of stimulation or energy is the mind. When the mind is free from the unnecessary waste of energy caused by meaningless thought processes and fallacious beliefs, it is full of its own energy; whereas the ordinary mind must depend entirely on food, money and material things for its stimulation.

2. Nothing should be eaten unless there are natural, vigorous hunger pangs. A simple sensation of relative emptiness is only psychological hunger and not a true guide to eating.

3. Food should be eaten slowly, chewed well and taken with awareness; one should pay full attention to the food and to the process of eating. Without this attention, eating the right quality and quantity of food is impossible, and proper assimilation cannot take place.

With moderate and balanced eating, the body can function properly, and a rejuvenation of body and mind can take place. If one leads a life of meditation—not a life of seclusion or inert samadhi, but the active meditation of understanding life from moment to moment—it is necessary to limit one's food strictly to the needs of the body, and not to make overeating the pleasure which it is for most people at present. It is then, and then alone, that the mind and body will be able to function in harmony. Perhaps then man will be free from such ailments as diabetes, high blood pressure, heart trouble, and the dreaded disease of cancer.

In physically active individuals, the appetite corresponds fairly accurately to the nutritional needs of the body; however, this mechanism does not operate in sedentary persons. Therefore sufficient daily exercise—an hour's walk at a speed of four to five miles per hour, or slow running for half an hour—is necessary to adjust organic functioning to a harmonious level.

Sleep and Dreams

Physiologists have not been able to clearly define the need for sleep and its mechanism. There are two common causes of sleep: the diminution of sensory stimulation, and excessive fatigue even in the presence of sensory stimulation. However, the question is: what part of the brain experiences fatigue and how much time does it require to recover from this fatigue? Even in sleep an electroencephalogram shows delta waves (up to 100 microvolts), demonstrating a certain degree of activity in the brain, although slow and infrequent.

It may be said that sleep is a habit, reflecting a very primitive inertia. As soon as mental activity stops and the mind becomes blank, it has a tendency to go to sleep. This is a very common early experience of meditators. Sleep can be warded off in a sitting posture if the neck is kept straight and erect and in line with the spine; but if the neck is bent or drooping, sleep is likely to supervene. If one becomes aware of the semi-awakened or hypnotic state between waking and sleeping, one can peep into the unconscious, and many psychic experiences and faculties can be developed in this way. Dr. Milan Rizyl of Czechoslovakia has used hypnosis to develop extra-sensory perception in his subjects.

In sleep the unconscious projects itself through varied symbols which we experience as dreams. The interpretation of these symbols or dreams can give us an insight into our unconscious mind. Some of these dreams may be prophetic in nature, and the vividness, light and hue of such dreams help to differentiate them

77

from other hazy and confused dreams. However, the interpretation of dreams is not the purpose of true meditation. The highest meditation aims at purifying the whole mind and eliminating the conflict between the conscious and the unconscious. With the ending of conflict there remains no need for dreams. A mind so free needs very few hours of dreamless sound sleep.

A highly energetic mind, which is free of conflict and which has transcended boredom, becomes free of its environment. It does not need stimulation, internal or external, in order to live a blissful, truly contented, balanced life.

> *"Yuktahara viharasya yuktacheshtasya karmasu, yuktaswapnavabodhasya yoga bhavati dukkha."*
> —Bhagavad Gita; Chapter V:17

> *"Yoga (integration which ends sorrow) is possible only for one who has a proper balance of eating and drinking, of activity, sleep and wakefulness."*

Surrender

Have you noticed that things sometimes come to you naturally, easily and spontaneously? You look, and you can see clearly. You listen, and you can listen with attention. You sit to meditate, and it seems so natural that you slip into the deepest recesses of your mind with ease. But then there come moments when you try and try very hard, and yet you cannot do it. What you thought was so easy now seems impossible. What are you going to do? You are disappointed and dejected—but what can you do? Can you do anything else? Have you left any stone unturned? No, you have reached the limit of your effort—the limit of your mind. Recognize this limit; admit your defeat. The moment you understand this limitation, the mind automatically becomes silent and still. This is surrender—but not a surrender to the will of God, for you do not know God, nor do you know his will. If you were so wise, you would need no book, no sadhana. Therefore, do not deceive yourself, but be simple and humble. Learn to recognize facts and learn to surrender to facts, because fundamentally you have no power to change a fact. You may try and try, but you cannot transcend the limit of your mind. Learn to surrender to the fact of your limitation. The moment you do it, what happens? Perhaps what you thought was so difficult, so impossible, yields and becomes possible. That is the magic of surrender. There is no barrier which you cannot cross with the art of surrender. Surrender does not mean accepting defeat permanently. There is no permanent defeat or victory, nor can there be a permanent surrender to any fact, because no fact is permanent. And surrender does not mean inertia, laziness and slothfulness; it means facing a fact squarely—seeing and feeling it completely—and in doing so going to that silence in which the Supreme Power is always waiting to operate. That power operates silently but surely, and as it moves one is revitalized, given a fresh mind, a new energy to move further and faster on the inner journey.

Surrender is not a compromise with the baser elements of your nature. It is the highest manifestation of intelligence on the human level. If you are tormented by the gnawing problem of some deviation in your nature, learn to be still and calm, and to surrender. Do not fritter away your energy in fighting it or in suppressing or sublimating it—that will lead you nowhere. Face it, feel it completely and then surrender to the activities of your mind without thinking of reform or modification. You will be surprised at the calm and peace that comes and at how the pulls and pressures melt away.

Here a problem may arise: surrender may happen just now, but the next moment the weakness or deviation again raises its head; it does not seem to be a lasting solution. This happens because you are not fully aware of the mechanism of the mind or perhaps because you are not very careful. But remember that what you can do once, you can do again. If you can solve a problem fundamentally and radically once, your mind will acquire a power or an energy which can do it again if need be. So you can live in this faith. Problems will always arise in life, but if you can solve one problem completely you will be able to solve all problems.

The greatest problem of the human mind is that it does not understand any problem fully. If you can give serious attention to understanding the problem, you will find that the very act of understanding is the solution of the problem. The physical action which may follow this understanding becomes a simple affair. The understanding of a problem is its solution; the understanding of a question is its answer. Nature is so benevolent and kind that it has placed the disease and its remedy, the problem and its solution, the question and its answer, very close together so that you do not have to struggle very hard. Pay full attention to a problem and the solution will come to you. To understand a problem completely, to frame a question correctly, is the act of highest intelligence. If you can do this you can lead an effortless, peaceful life even in a violent, insane, and chaotic world. Then alone will you discover that freedom is, essentially, to be free of environment and to live unaffected by it.

There is a story about Lord Shiva and his two sons, Ganesha and Kartikeya. The sons decided that whichever of the two could complete the circle of the three worlds earlier would be acknowledged the greater. Kartikeya had a fast means of transport, and started at once on this race. Ganesha had a slow means of transport and so he recognized the futility of attempting the race; he simply circled his father Lord Shiva thrice and sat down quietly. When Kartikeya returned exhausted and panting, Ganesha announced that Kartikeya had lost the race. He explained that since Lord Shiva was the Lord of the Universe, his circling around him was equivalent to going around the whole universe. Ganesha is thus the Lord of Intelligence, according to Hindu mythology, for wisdom lies in understanding one's limitation and surrendering to the fact of one's helplessness. Hectic, senseless activity, with its attendant inner turmoil, will lead us nowhere. To make real progress in our spiritual journey, we have to learn the art of surrender. It is not through rituals, practices, and outer disciplines that truth can be realized. Know your limitations and learn to surrender, and truth will come to you unsought. Similarly, do not seek siddhis or miracles. If you have learnt the art of surrender and can go into silence, these powers may seek you—but perhaps at that level they will even become meaningless and insignificant to you.

The beauty of this art is that you may reach the highest pinnacle of spiritual wisdom, but ego will not touch you, for you know that whatever you are is the result of surrender and not of any practice. Humility will not leave you even at the greatest height, for in humility alone can true virtue blossom.

You may reach the highest point of the intuitive or psychic plane by pursuing certain methods or contemplation, but no method whatever can take you out of the psychic plane. In the esoteric language of kundalini yoga, you may go up to the seventh chakra (*sahasrar* or the thousand-petalled lotus in the crown of the head) or the seventh plane (*sat loka*) in this way. This is a plane of positivity which may be represented by pure white (the synthesis of the seven colors of the spectrum). You may find powers or siddhis and great self-satisfaction, but pure love and bliss cannot be experienced here. The seventh plane is the highest point of the shell of the human mind and no effort, however hard, can break it. Beyond this no method, no discipline, no guru can take you. Only through the silent meditation of observation can you realize that all that your mind has experienced or can project into the future, is limited and cannot lead to freedom. In this negative state—which can be compared to the eighth plane of consciousness—all the powers and siddhis disappear and your mind is only aware of silence. Now can you stay with this silence, this negative state, and completely give up any hope, desire or image of beyond—all hope even of *mukti* or freedom? This is surrender, the supreme vehicle which can take you beyond the shell of *I* and *me*. Surrender and patience are the two ingredients which when combined bring about the biggest explosion, much larger and stronger than any nuclear explosion. This in turn brings about a total transformation of the human mind, illuminating it with the flame of love, which is at once both human and divine.

Thus you will see that silent meditation is the shortest and the safest route to the highest spiritual realm, free from the dangers of the psychic realm with its attendant powers and siddhis. It is the easiest approach if you are earnest and serious and want to discover the highest truth, meaning, and significance of life.

For total integration, however, one must look into the deepest recesses of the unconscious mind—the psychic or intuitive plane—as outlined in the chapter on the highest concept. While going through this plane it is advisable not to become caught in the net of powers and siddhis. These powers and siddhis may come to you, may follow you, but you should not chase them. Only then can you maintain your humility. In humility alone can love blossom; love and power seldom co-exist. Every power, save the power of love, is a frictional energy. Only in the power of love— the supreme power—do conflict and friction cease to exist.

You may have notions about love, or read many definitions of love, but all this is not love. The explosion that takes place in silence, within you, is love—and it defies all definitions, all explanations. The light of this explosion may last a moment, hours, or days, depending upon your previous preparation or your simplicity. But once it comes, it takes such a grip on you that although you may slide down into your old mechanical mind if you are not careful, you cannot go back to it permanently. You will only increase your misery and suffering if you do not say goodbye to it. You have no choice, no alternative left but to proceed—slowly or quickly—to the highest summit. Choice came to you in the transitory period of your evolution and gave you a possibility of freedom and a sense of responsibility. There is no choice for the animal except to follow its instincts. There is no choice for a man who has gone beyond the shell of his ego. There is only a play of divine nature without any alternative.

You may advance sufficiently, but as you are never conscious of your progress—since the yardstick of the ego is missing here—you may on occasion be haunted by memories of your past, your half-animal, half-human existence. You have to observe these memories and experience them so fully that ultimately no residue from your past remains and you enter a domain where you are not interested in freedom nor even understanding. Just as siddhis followed you, now freedom also follows you. And if you do not make the mistake of identifying yourself with this Supreme Power—which would mean a hindered movement on your journey—you will find that there is only a divine movement, no observer or observed, lover or beloved.

This is the stage of highest devotion, or *parabhakti*, in which there is no adored. This is the highest stage of knowledge and understanding, where both merge in the ocean of love. If you began with an insatiable discontent and seriousness, you will not rest content even at this summit. Since you are now interested neither in understanding nor in freedom, and you do not want to identify yourself with anything, the way will open for you to pass into a stage where there is neither pleasure nor pain—no experience. It is a frightful thing to imagine, but one of the most beautiful things to actually experience: this transition from experience to non-experience.

There is no road to the highest summit or *maha shunya*, except surrender and patience—no path, no system but the ending of all paths and methods. This is the supreme moment in which all authority ends and all scriptures become meaningless—or full of their real meaning. You do not need any book or guru now. Now divinity breathes through you. Eating, drinking and walking become the highest miracles.

Epilogue

Reality is in a state of flux and is ever changing; it is the product of intensity translated through thought or imagination. But intensity cannot be created by thought—it comes only out of clear perception. The drive created by thought or desire is not intensity but the energy of conflict. So perception is the reservoir of true intensity. Every perception has to be lived totally to transform it into reality. When it is not so lived, perception becomes an intellectual formulation and only causes modification in consciousness. Each level of reality, which is a conscious realization of perception, has to be lived completely before the mind can open up to the possibility of another level of reality. The totally transformed consciousness has the pliability and flexibility of shifting from one level of reality to another in quick succession—in order to relate to the conditioned reality outside, or in order to transform it. Only when the mind can relate to the social challenge and respond completely to it, can it be said that the basis of total transformation has been laid.

The transformation on the intellectual level appears to be an act of perception, and is timeless, but when the energy of transformation acts upon the emotional or psychic level and the physical level, a process in time seems to set in. This process may be long and drawn out or short, depending upon the openness and receptivity of the psyche and body. But it has to be clearly understood that for the process to proceed smoothly and speedily, psychological time must come to an end completely. The mind which is undergoing changes has to live in the eternal now, and obliterate all projections of the goal and future images in order for total manifestation of this timeless energy to take place in the psyche and the body.

As the process proceeds, new faculties and capacities manifest in the mind, and the body becomes progressively free of disease, disharmony, decay and aging. Each and every body and brain cell is striving towards survival. This urge for survival, for which psychological and physical security is needed, is an expression of immortality. When the psyche has gone beyond division between 'me' and 'you', between the individual and the world around, it goes beyond psychological hurt. The conflict in the psyche which manifests as envy, jealousy, competition and violence is the basis of psychological hurt. When the psyche is free of conflict, a wholeness is reflected in the body; the body gradually becomes incapable of being hurt, sick or disabled. Timelessness is reflected in the body as the slowing down or abolition of the aging process. The body may survive for indefinitely long periods of time, or newer mutations in the body may manifest.

Technologically, through transplants and other bio-medical means, man is attempting to conquer disease and aging; he is looking forward to a period of near-immortality of the body in the not distant future. However, in achieving this end through technology, dependence on artificial means of support and sustenance is not ended. And therefore this dependence, coupled with a fear of boredom, will make a mockery of immortality. This so-called immortality will be akin to the immortality of plastic—a purely mechanical existence. But when change is brought about by a transformation in consciousness, immortality first manifests in the psyche and then in the body. Then and then alone can a total transformation of the human personality—true immortality—manifest. Then immortality is not only survival of the body, but the emergence of a new human being and social order.

Truth is timeless and immutable—whereas reality is bound by

time and space; created, maintained, and modified by thought and imagination. When reality is created by thought through techniques, such a reality reflects the imperfections and limitations of thought. When the transformed consciousness creates reality through intelligence, although thought is still used as an instrument, the resultant reality does not reflect the limitation and disorder so common to thought-created reality. So the transformed consciousness creates different levels of functional reality appropriate to the needs of its expression. Such a mind is a creator of reality, not a slave to it.

We are all creators of reality through thought and imagination, but when we so create, that reality is fraught with fear and anxiety, and enslaves us. When the transformed mind creates reality through intelligence, that pure reality is free of fear and does not lead to bondage. Then such a reality is only functional, and is dissolved by the transformed mind when necessary. Thus while living in reality, the mind remains free.

So a free mind is not divorced from reality, nor does it escape from it; it transforms it and adds to it when necessary. Freedom or moksha, without the power to create this pure reality, is only intellectual, sterile and meaningless. But this freedom to create reality, this immense creative power only manifests out of the ashes of the ego. A mind still cluttered with choices and preferences, which is not totally one with the universe, does not touch upon this summit. Only when all choices have come to an end can the mind begin upon the journey to this summit, which lies beyond time and space. This is the supreme sacrifice which the ego must make before the altar of truth so that true individuality may emerge.

Glossary

Adishankara	founder of Advaita or non-dualistic philosophy; a great scholar & yogi of the eighth century credited with uprooting Buddhism from India
anahat nada	inner subtle sounds
aparabhakti	lower form of devotion wherein duality persists
Ardhanarishwara	form of Indian God (Shiva) which is half male & half female
Aurobindo, Shri (1872-1950)	a great Indian seer, poet & nationalist
avatars	incarnations of God
bala	a child
bhakti yoga	yoga of devotion
Brahman	Supreme creative energy
Buddha (C. 6th c. B.C.)	founder of Buddhism
Chaitanya Maha Prabhu (1485-1533)	a great Indian mystic, the "God-intoxicated preacher," believed to be the incarnation of Lord Vishnu
darshan	to see; philosophy
Gautama Muni (C. 6th c. B.C.)	the chief disciple of Lord Mahavira, the founder of Jainism. A contemporary of Buddha

Gita (Bhagavad Gita)	a religious book of the Hindus
gurus	spiritual teachers
ishtadevata	personal deity; one's highest image
jada	dull or inert
japa	a form of meditation in which beads are counted to the repetition of a mantra
jivan mukti	state of salvation or liberation in one's lifetime
jnana yoga	yoga of knowledge
karma	Sanskrit term for the law of cause and effect; the result of an action from the past or from a past life
karma yoga	yoga of action
Krishnamurti, Jiddu (1895-)	contemporary thinker and speaker on the nature of the mind and human intelligence
Lao-Tzu (C. 6th c. B.C.)	first philosopher of Chinese Taoism
Mahavira, Lord (C. 599-527 B.C.)	Indian reformer; founder of Jainism according to Western scholars. Contemporary of the Buddha
Mahamaya	female aspect of the Supreme Power
maha shunya	the Great Void or silence
Maha vakyas	the great aphorisms
mantra	a mystical formula; a sound either voiced or silent
Mirabei	a famous woman devotee of Lord Krishna
moksha	liberation or freedom
neti-neti	"not this, not this"

Natraj Shiva	Lord Shiva in his form as the king of dancers
nirvana	the great void or silence
nirvikalp samadhi	state of self-absorption or trance in which there is no thought at all
nirvikalp jnana	state of non-verbal or pure perception
padmasana	lotus posture
parabhakti	supreme devotion wherein there is a state of non-duality
paramahamsa	a liberated or enlightened being
Param Shiva	supreme aspect of Lord Shiva
Patanjali (dates unknown)	expounder of the original philosophy of yoga
Pundit Nimai	a scholar named Nimai who became Chaitanya Maha Prabhu, the famous mystic
pishacha	a ghost; an evil spirit
Ramana Maharshi (1879-1950)	Hindu philosopher & yogi, proponent of self-enquiry
sadhaka	a spiritual aspirant
sadhana	a way of aspiration; spiritual pursuit
samadhi	a conflict-free state: a state of self-absorption or trance
Sankhya	philosophy of understanding through analysis
Sanskrit	ancient language of the Hindus
savikalpa jnana	knowledge in which thought remains (recognition and naming)

savikalpa samadhi	a state of samadhi in which some thought process persists
Shakti	creative or positive energy; female counterpart of Lord Shiva
Shiva	negative energy; Hindu Lord of the Universe, the god of destruction.
Shiva Lingam	symbol of creativity
Siddhartha	childhood name of Lord Buddha; the hero of a novel of the same name by Hermann Hesse
siddhasana	a yogic posture (the half-lotus position)
siddhi	power or perfection; psychic power
Soor Das	name of a great devotee of Lord Krishna
swabhava	innate nature
swadharma	expression of innate nature
tantric	pertaining to the philosophy of Tantra, in which symbols are freely used
Tripur Sundari	beauty of the three worlds; tantric name of the Supreme Energy
Tulsidas (c.1543-1623)	Indian poet; author of the sacred book Ramayana in Hindi
unmata	crazy
Upanishadic	pertaining to the Upanishads, sacred literature of the post-Vedic period
Vam Marg	left-handed path; a system of tantra in which sex and drugs were freely used
yoga	union or integration
yogi	a master of yogic discipline; an integrated person

ABOUT THE AUTHOR

Dr. R. P. KAUSHIK was born in India in 1926. His search for understanding began early in life with the death of a school companion. No intellectual approach offered a satisfactory answer, and it became clear that no experience-direct or indirect-could ever offer a total solution. Gradually all ideas and images dropped away and he was led to the discovery that reality can only be perceived and understood from moment to moment.

Dr. Kaushik studied and practiced medicine for twenty-three years, until 1973, at which time contact increased with people interested in exploring this movement of life beyond beliefs, systems, and techniques. Over the following years he traveled and met with those who wished to share his perception, and wrote six books before his death in 1981.

Sentient Publications, LLC publishes books on cultural creativity, experimental education, transformative spirituality, holistic health, new science, and ecology, approached from an integral viewpoint. Our authors are intensely interested in exploring the nature of life from fresh perspectives, addressing life's great questions, and fostering the full expression of the human potential. Sentient Publications' books arise from the spirit of inquiry and the richness of the inherent dialogue between writer and reader.

We are very interested in hearing from our readers. To direct suggestions or comments to us, or to be added to our mailing list, please contact:

SENTIENT PUBLICATIONS, LLC
1113 Spruce Street
Boulder, CO 80302
303.443.2188
contact@sentientpublications.com
www.sentientpublications.com